FLORAL DELIGHTS COLORING COLLECTION

WEDDING CAKES EDITION

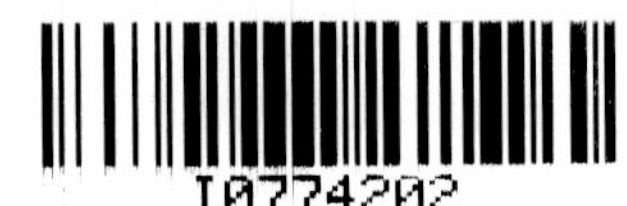

33 COLORING PAGES +DARK AND LIGHT VERSION INCLUDED

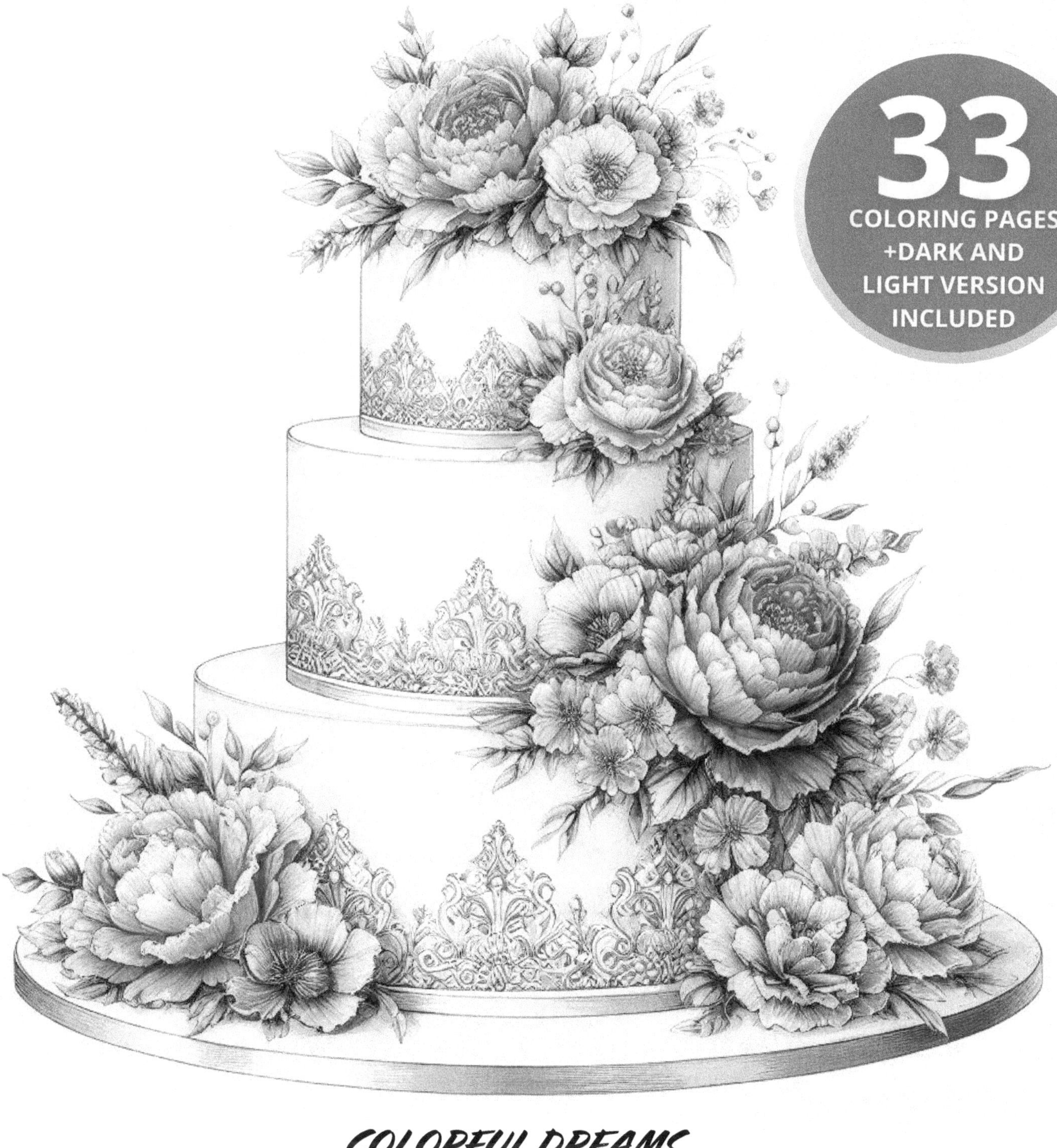

COLORFUL DREAMS

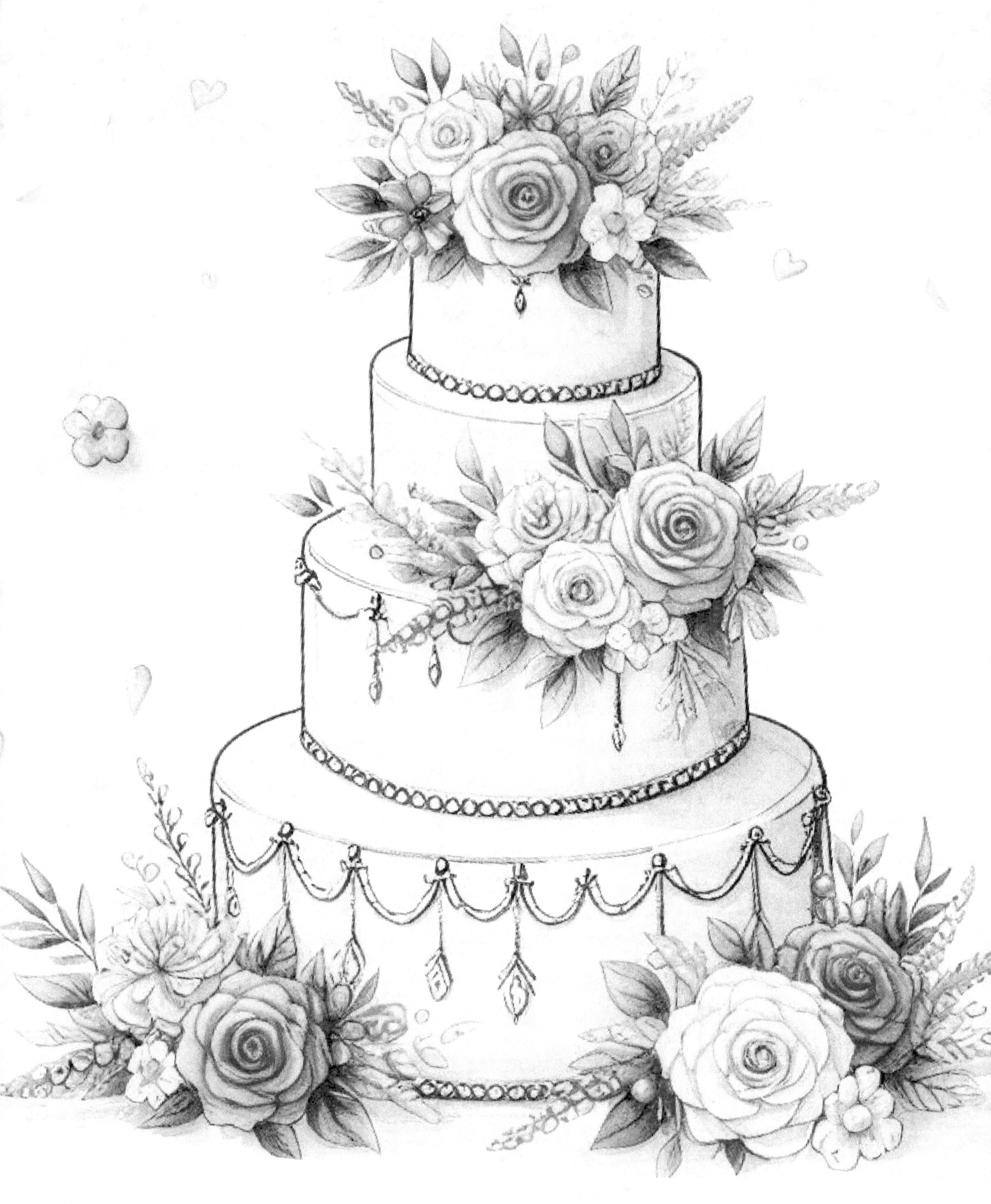

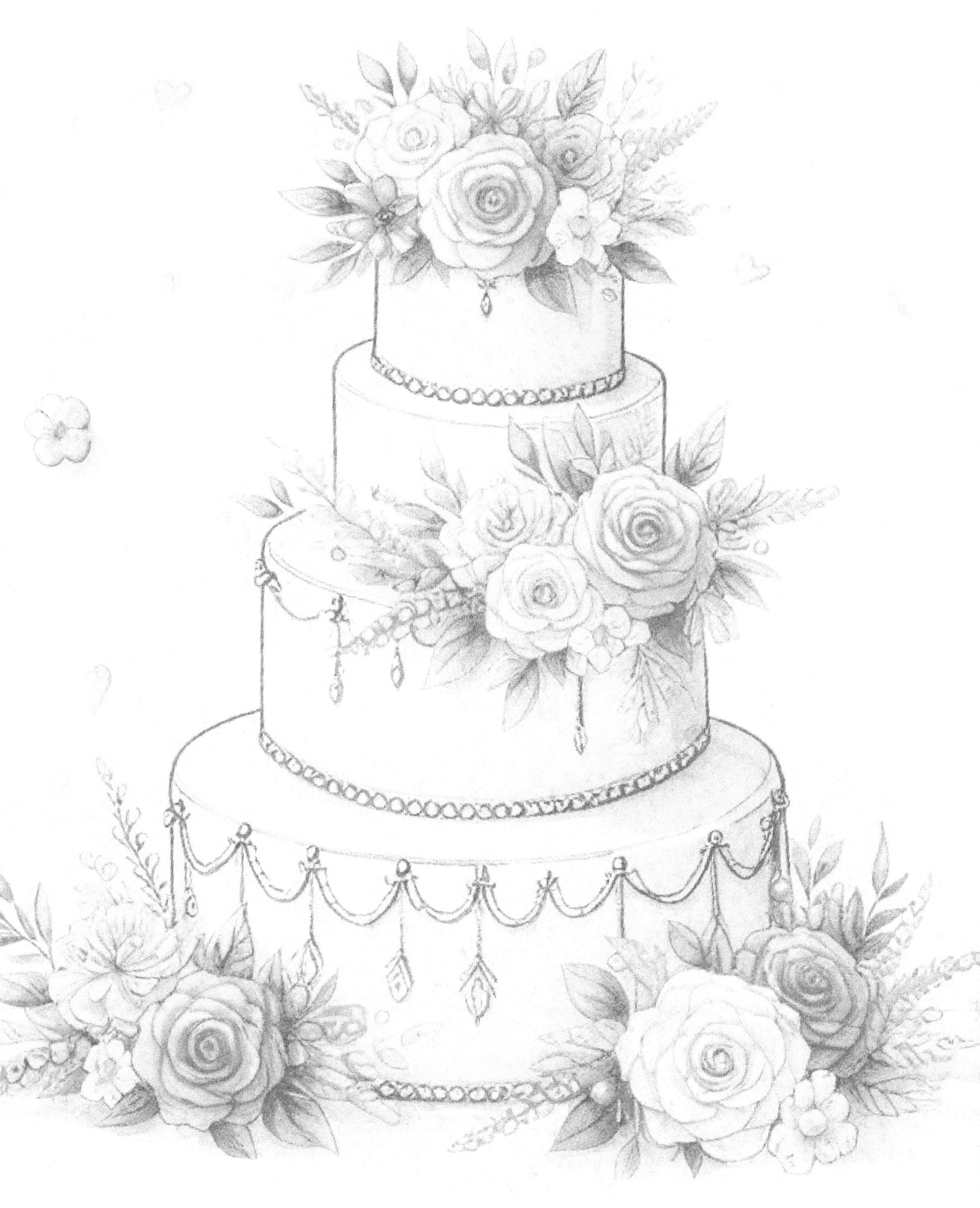

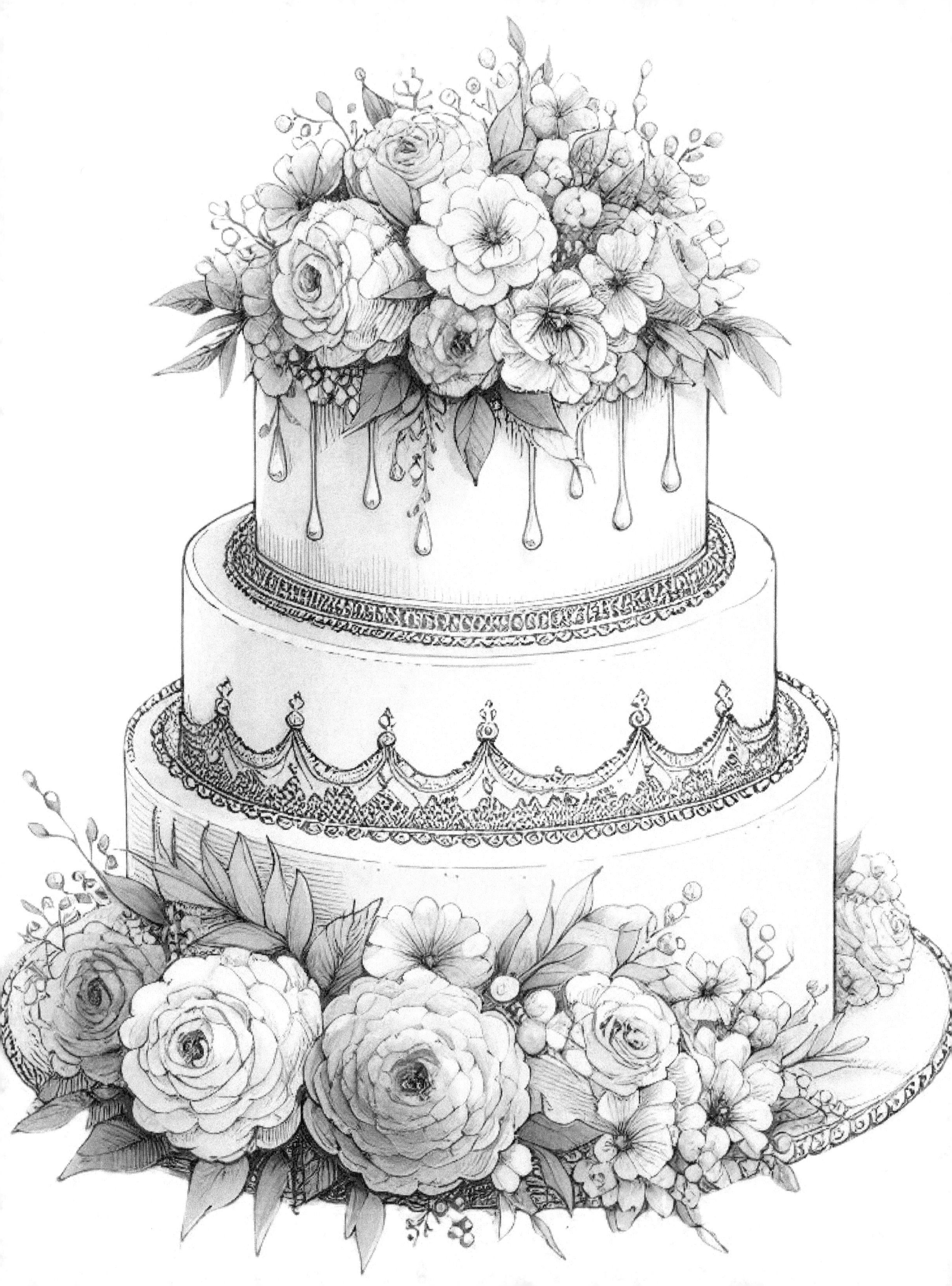

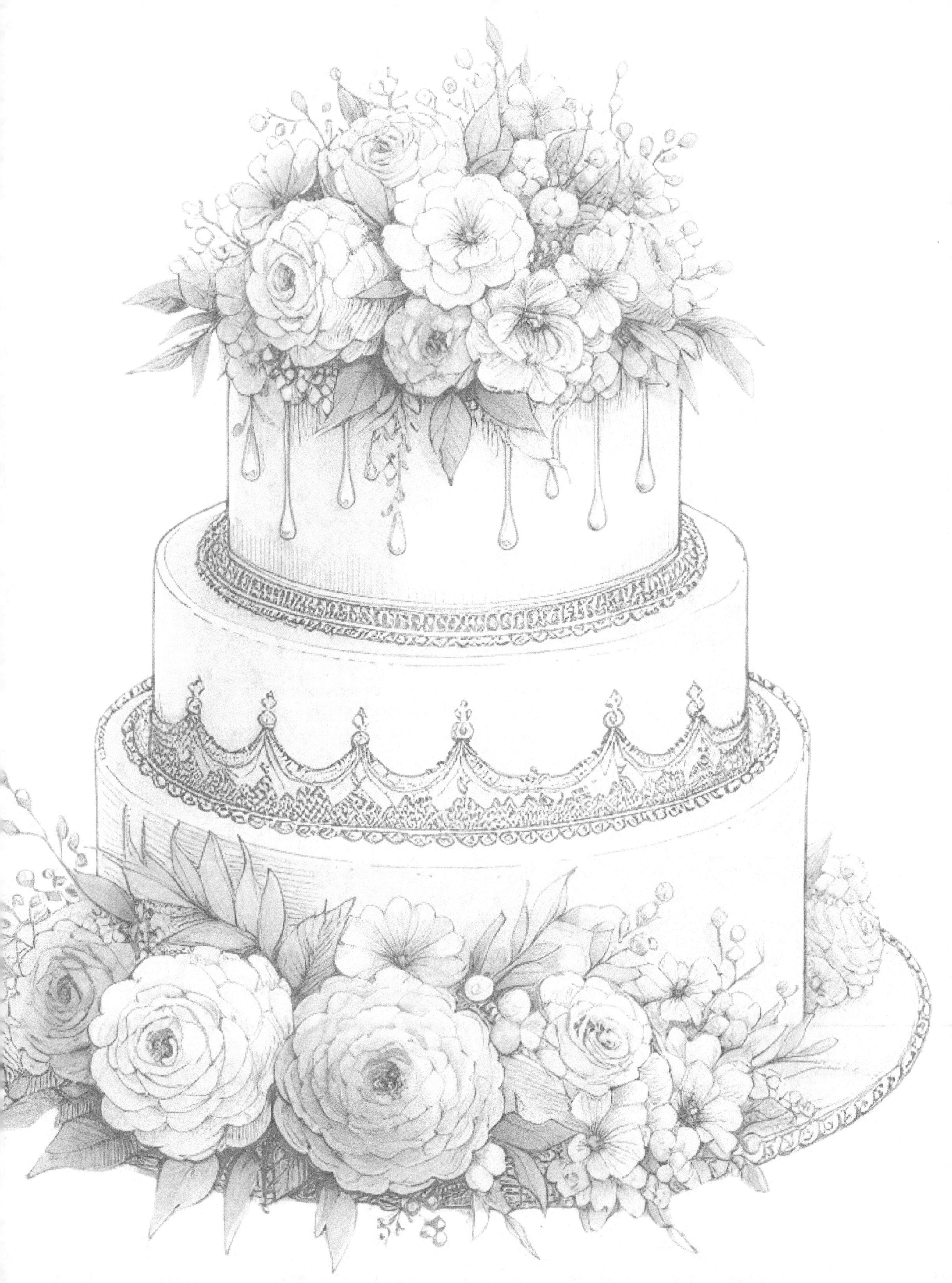

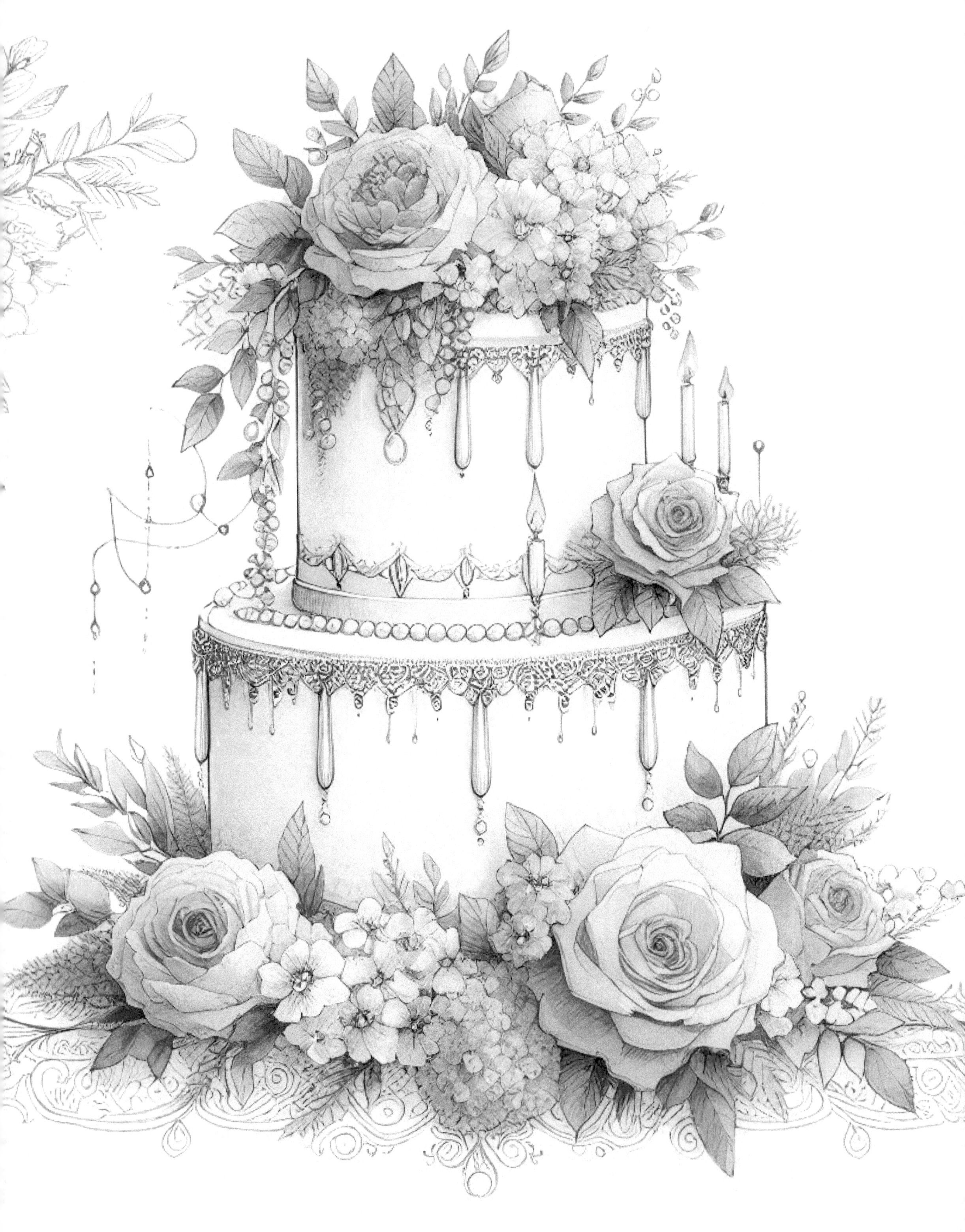

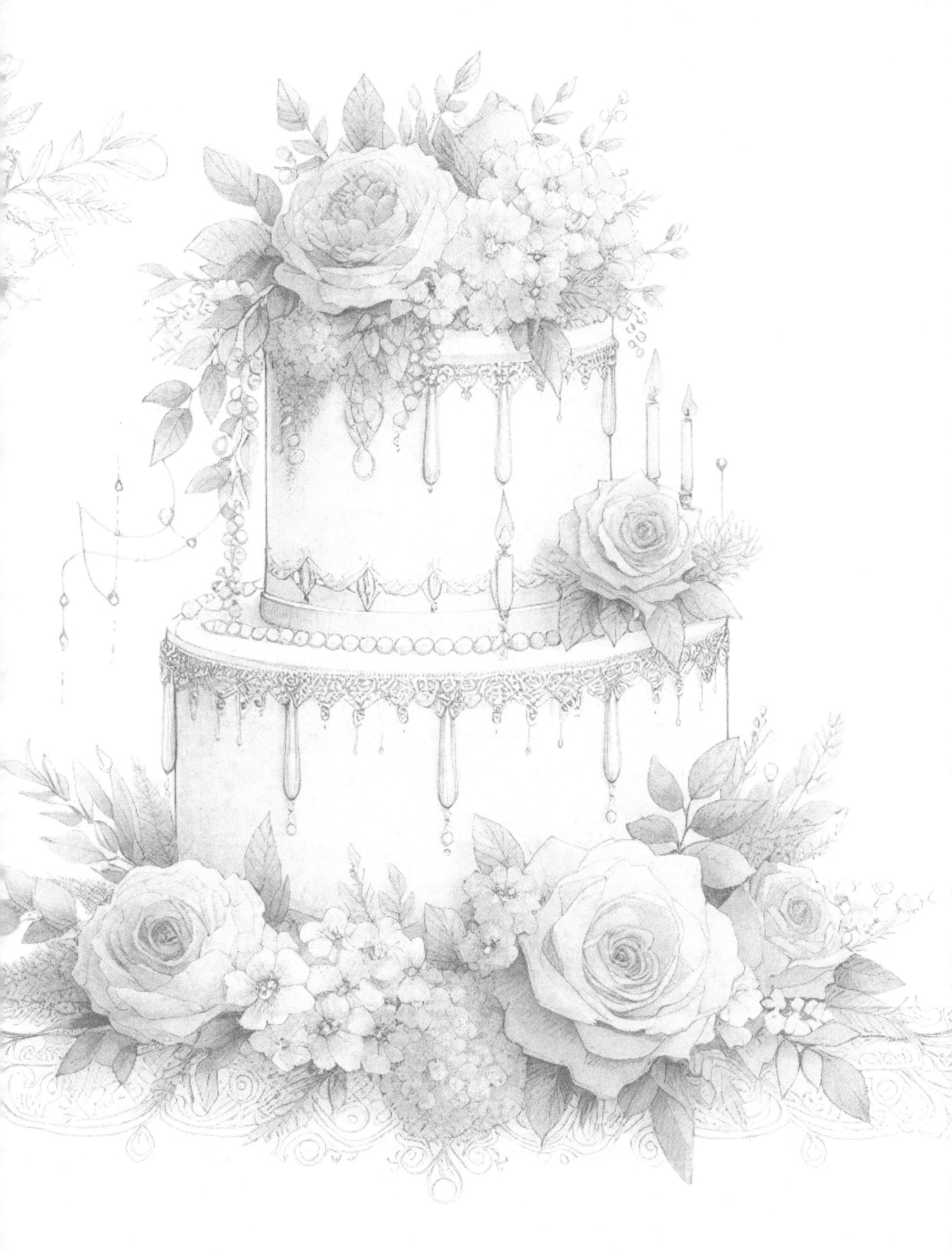

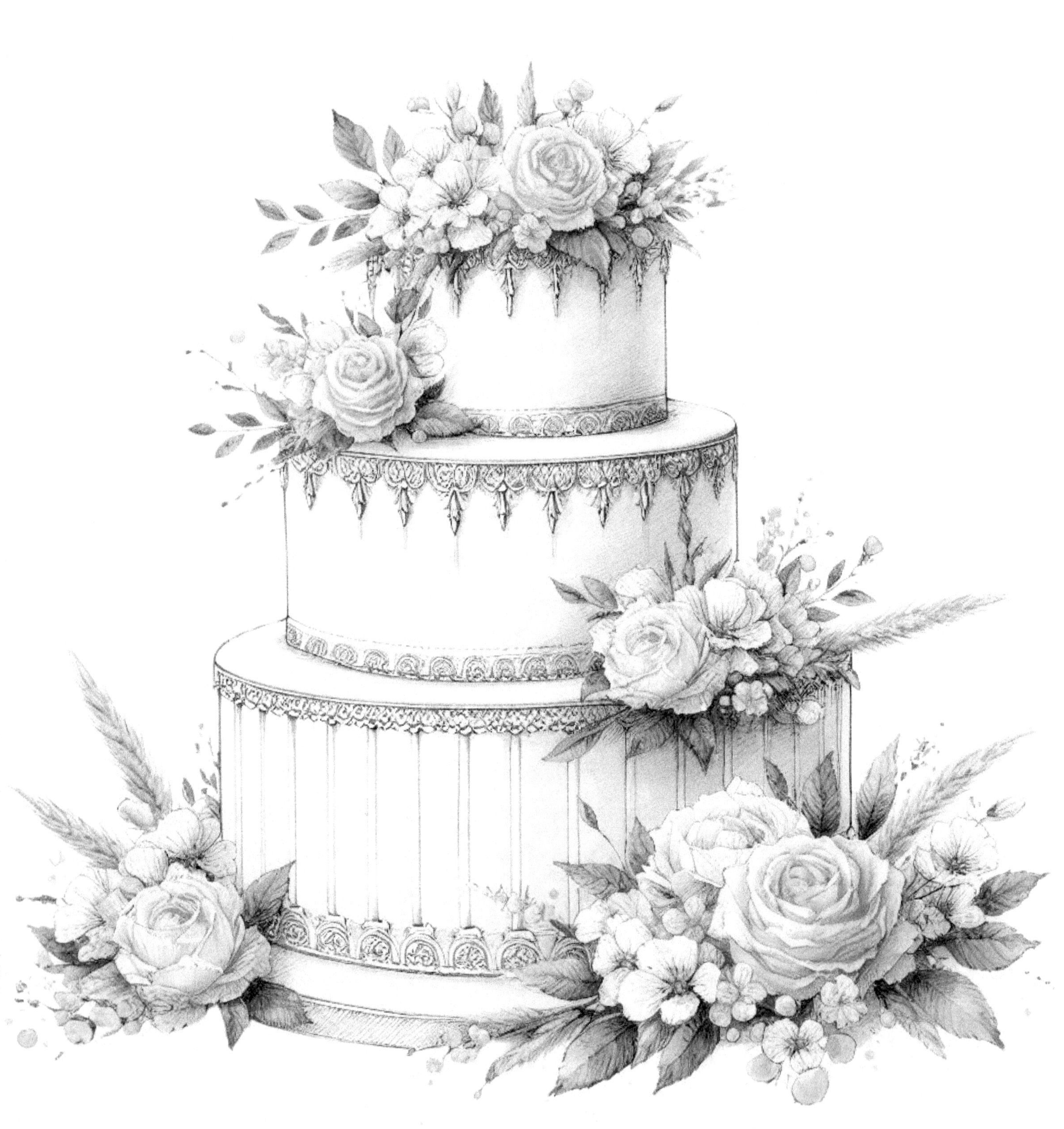

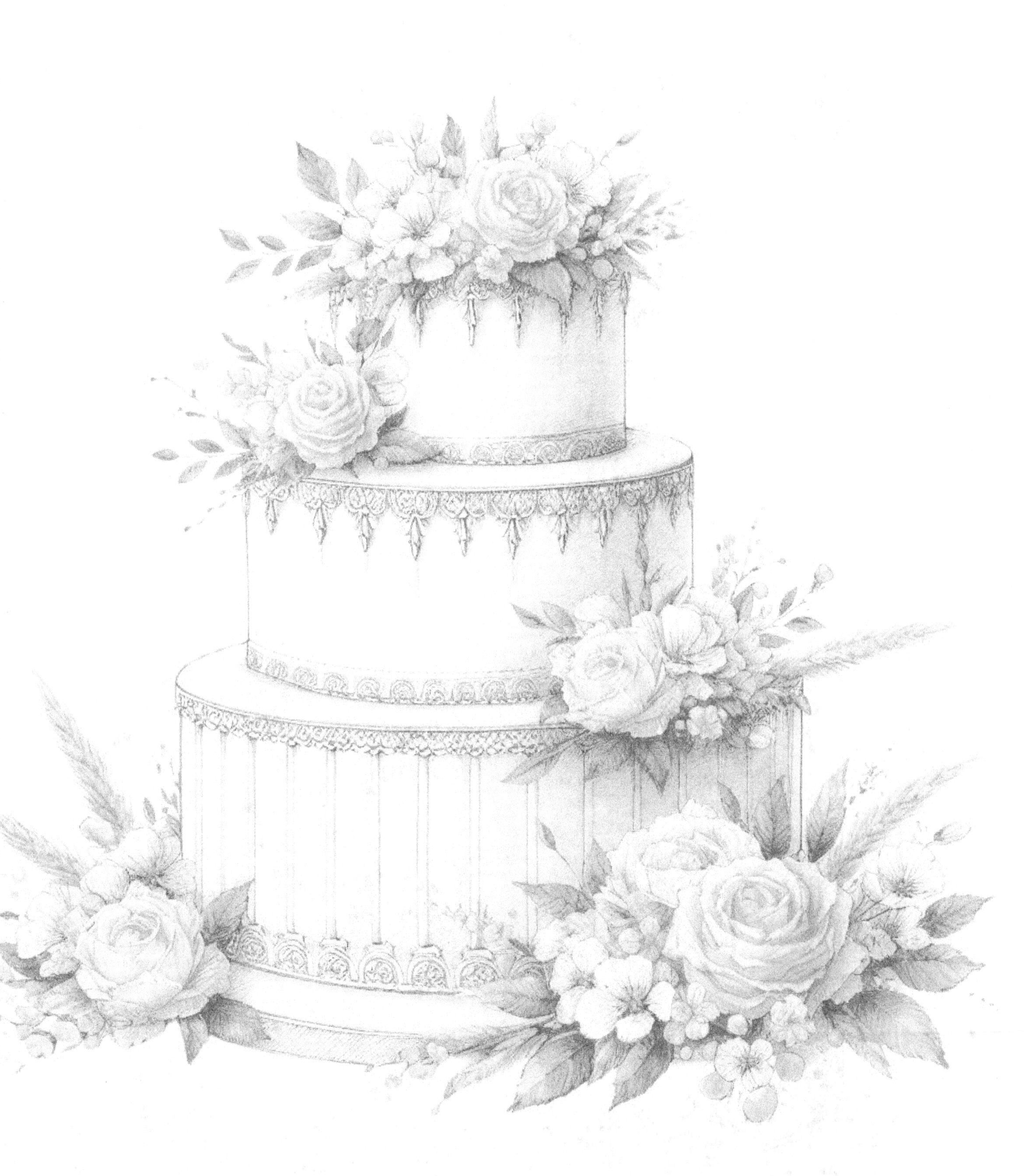

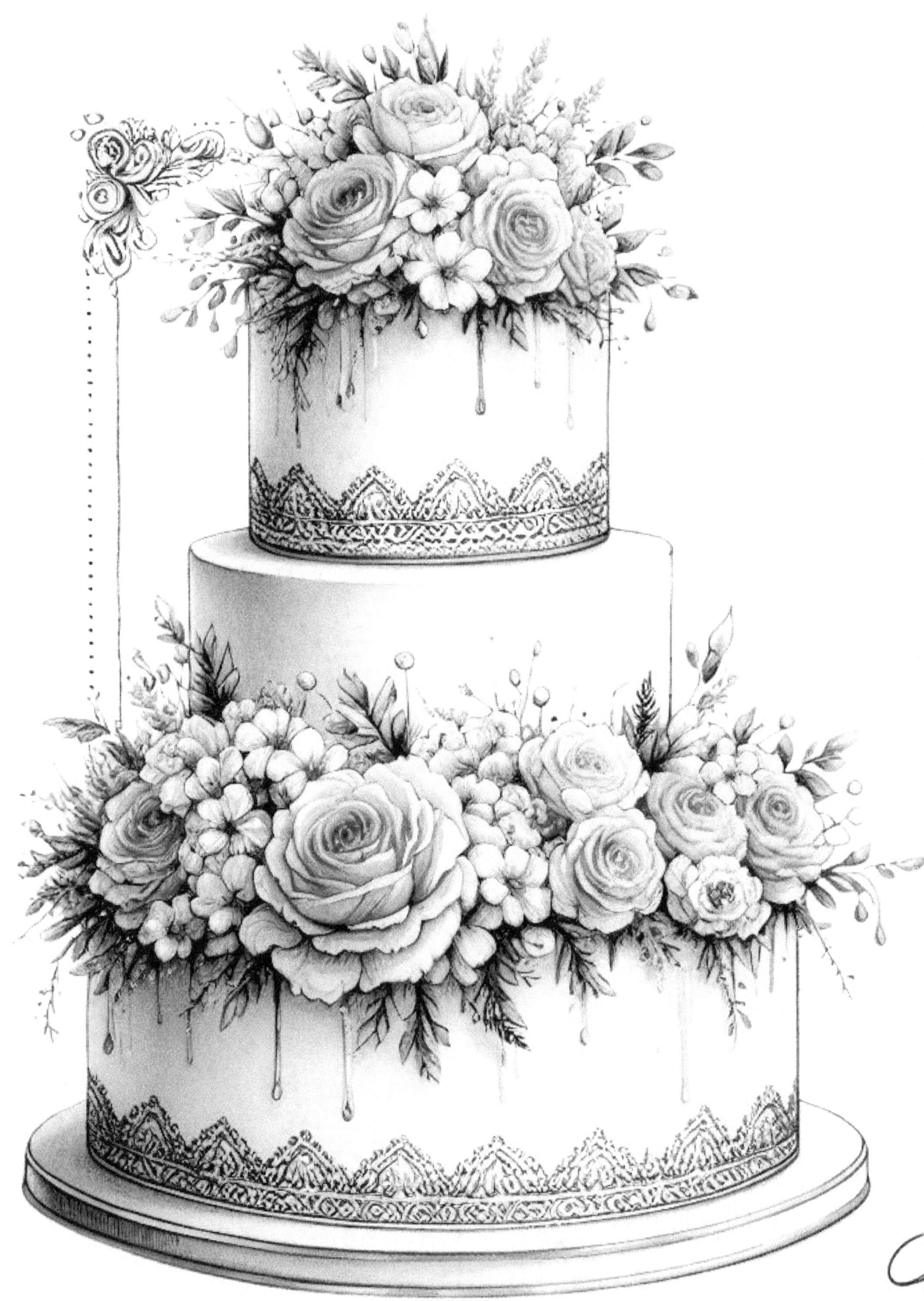

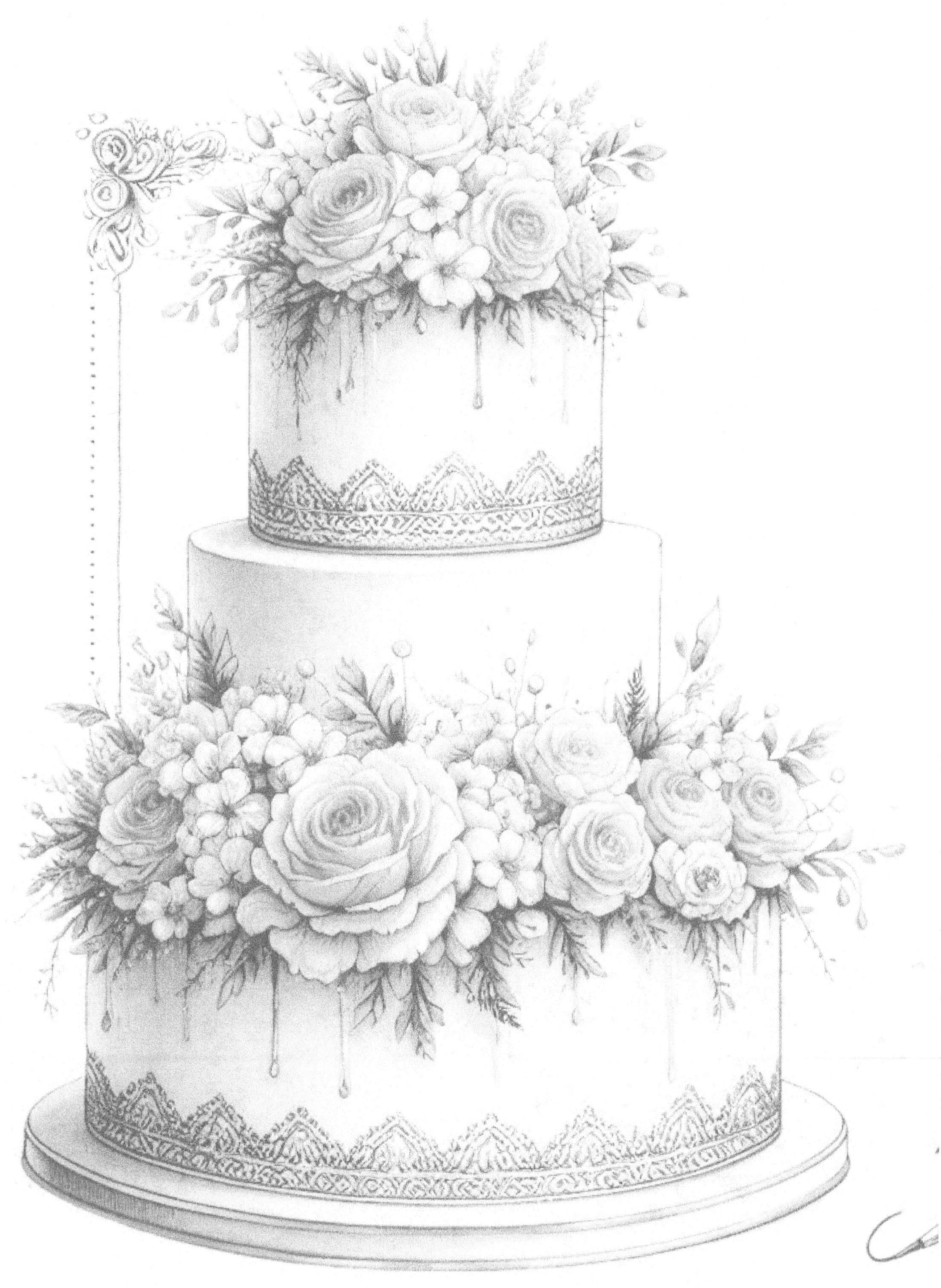

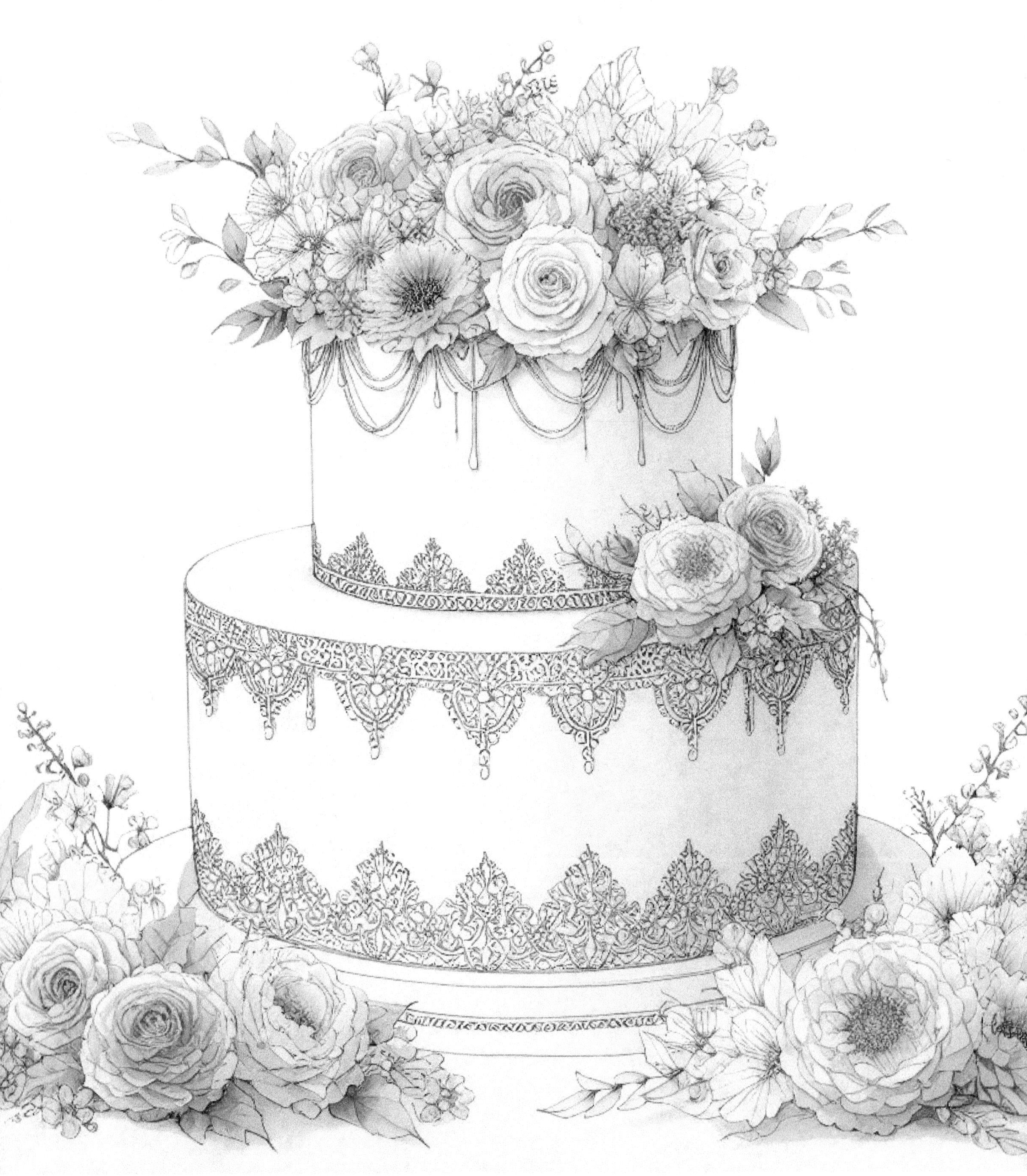

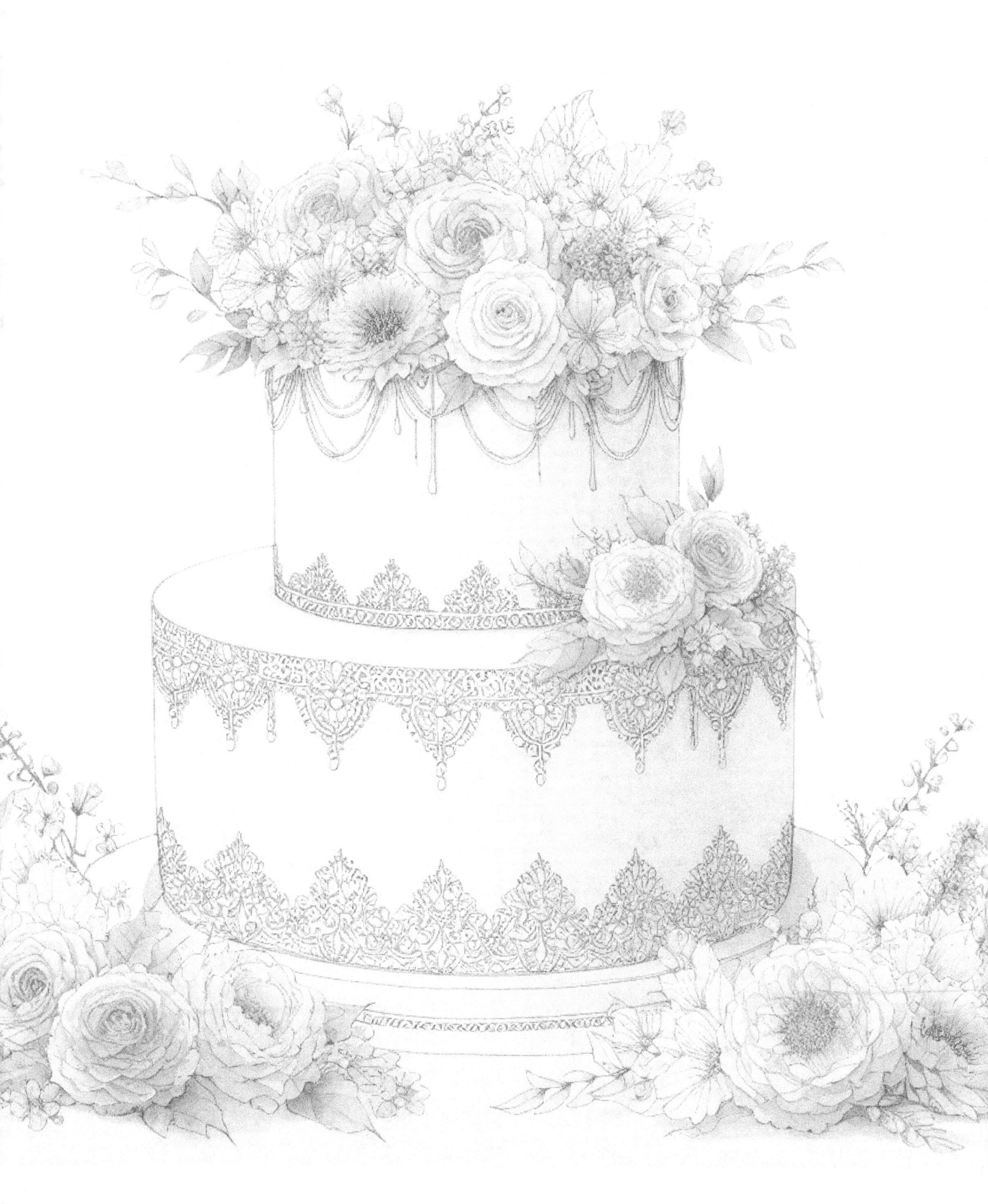

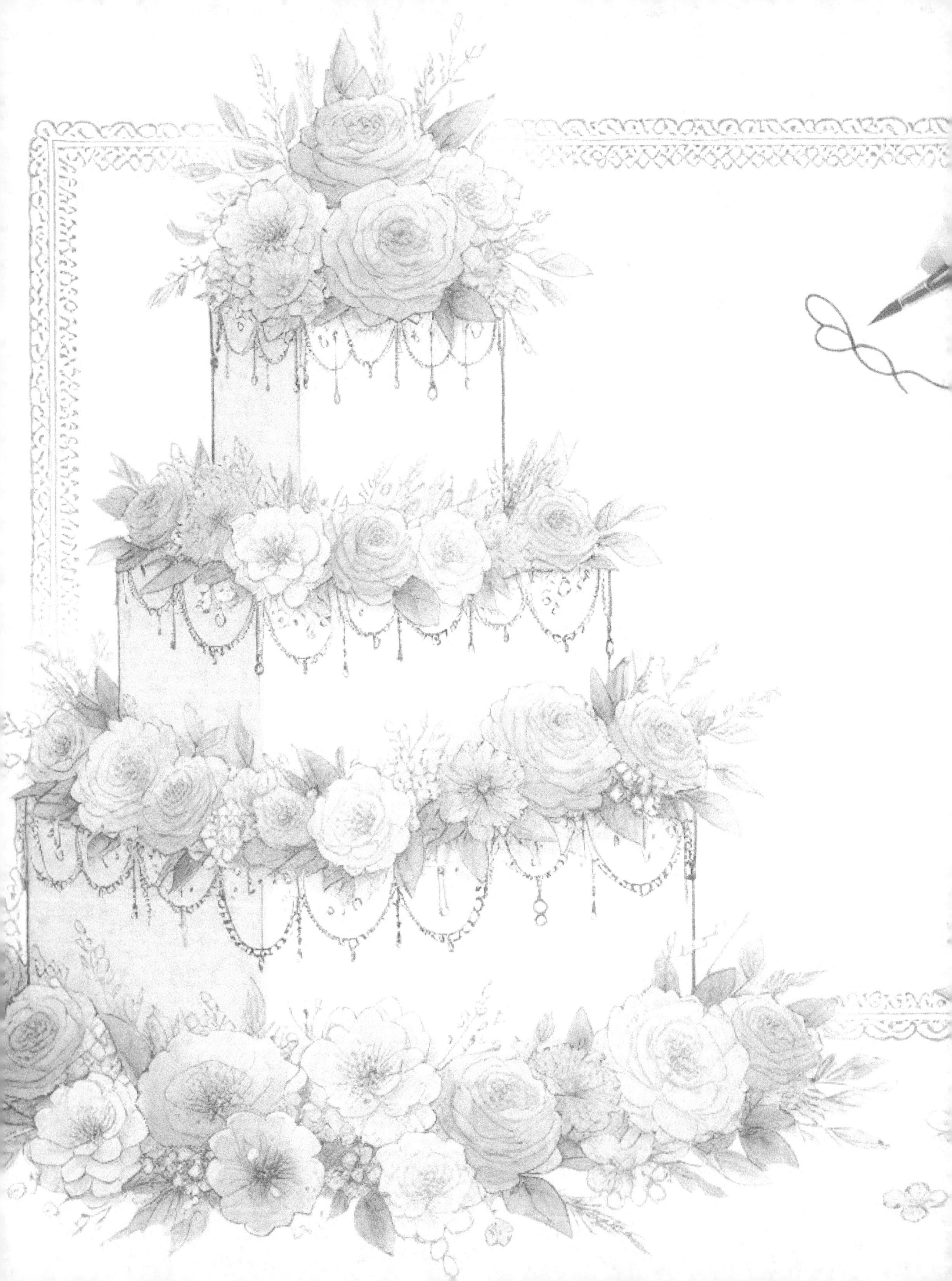

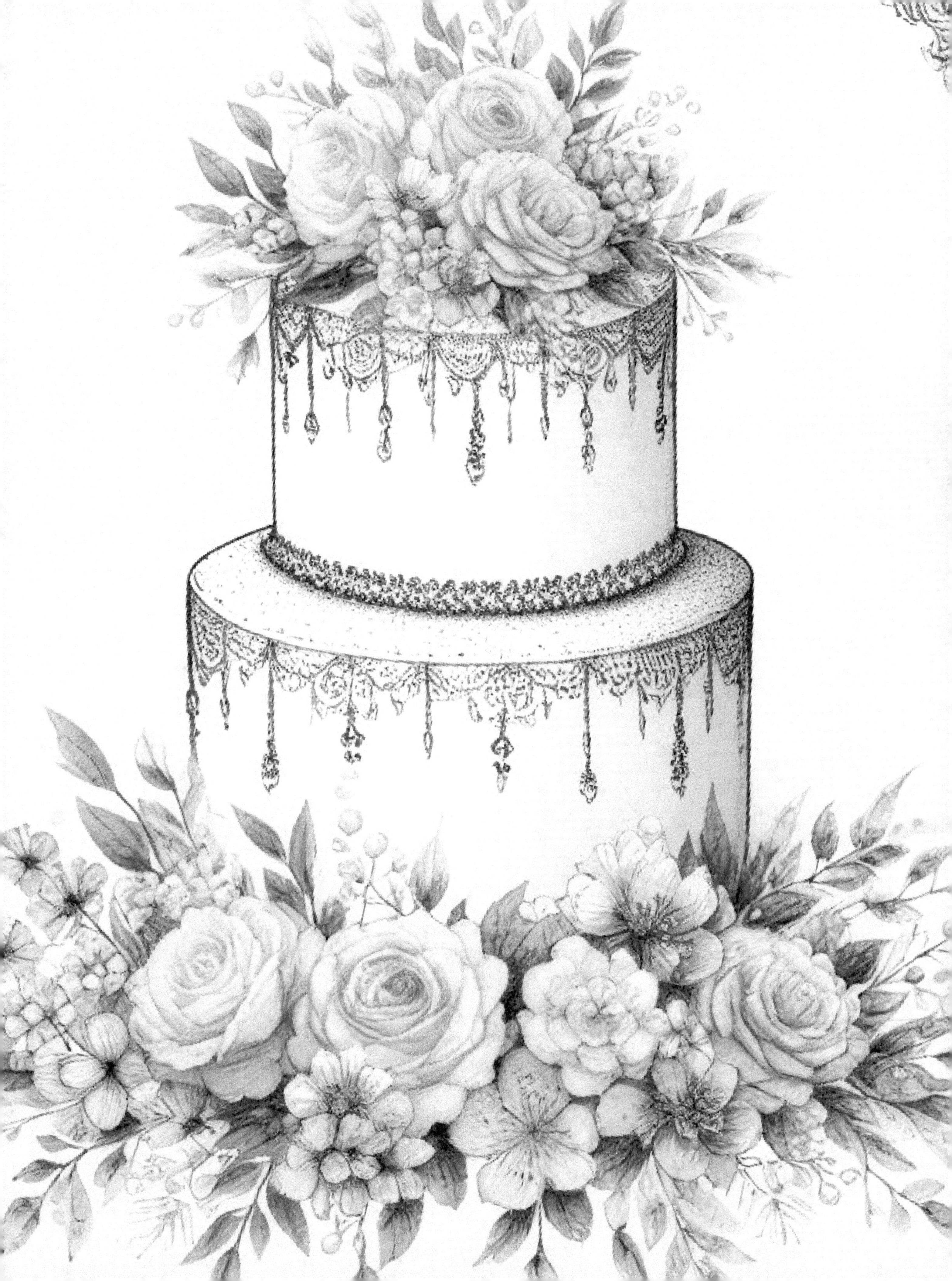

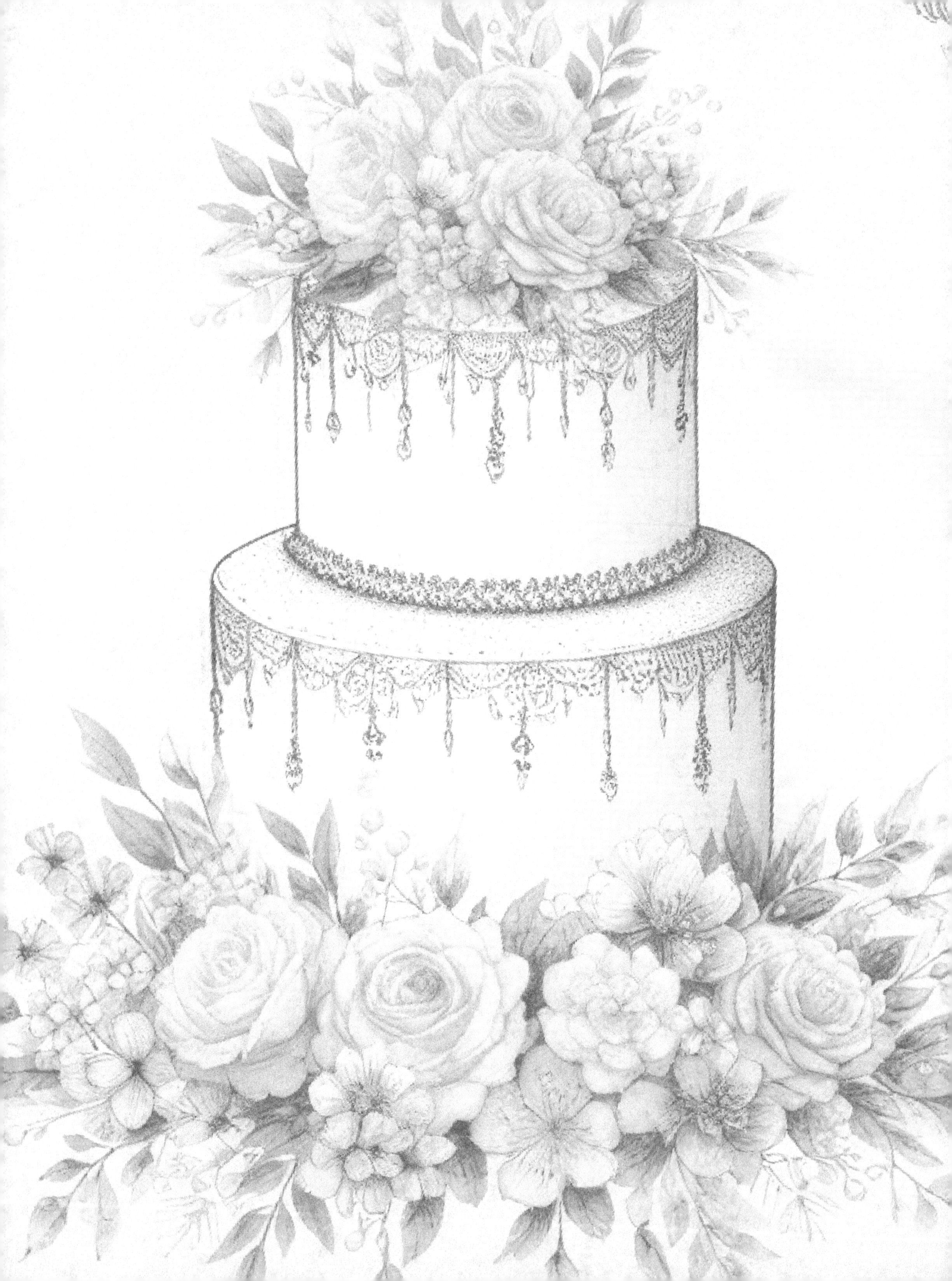

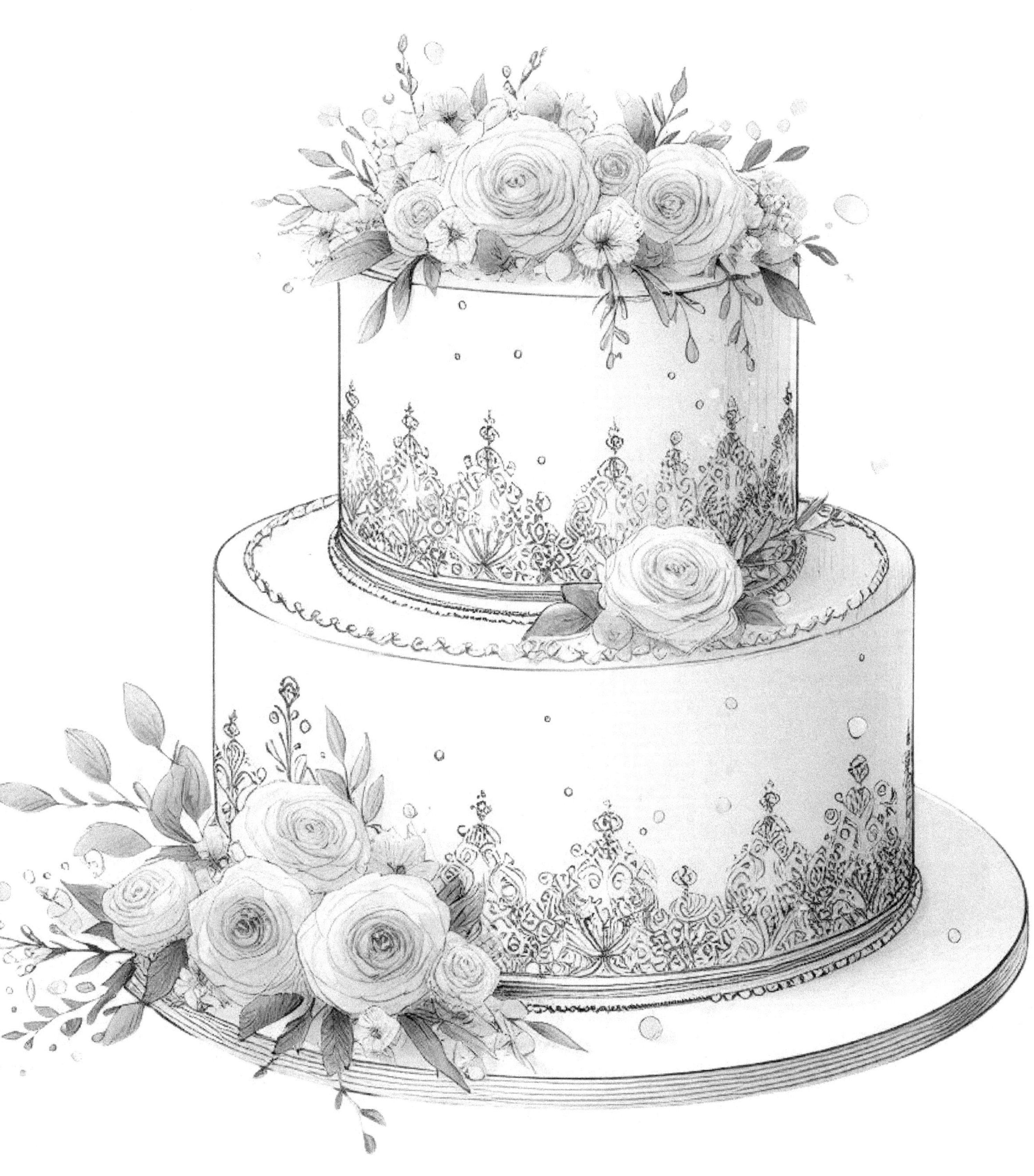

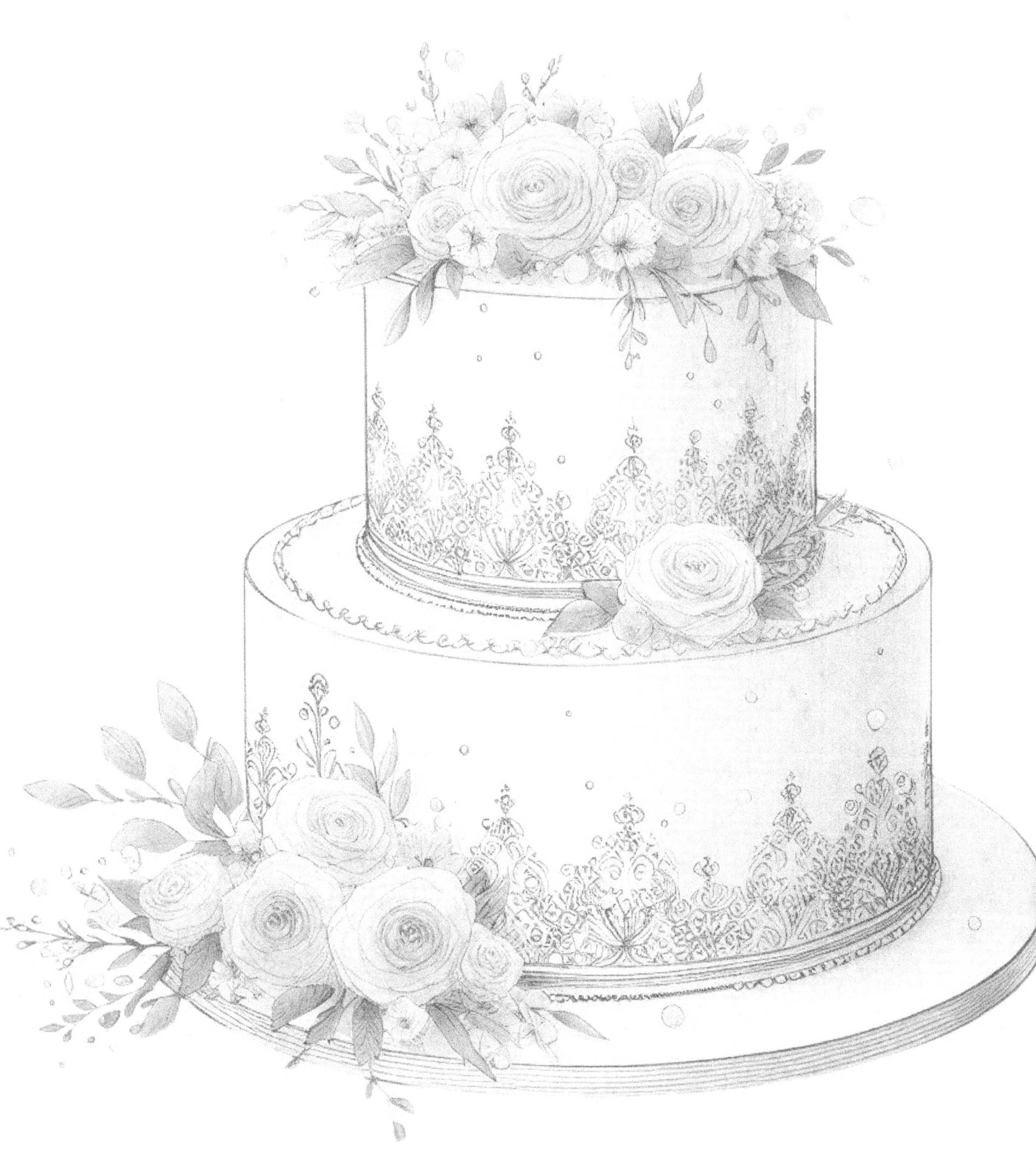

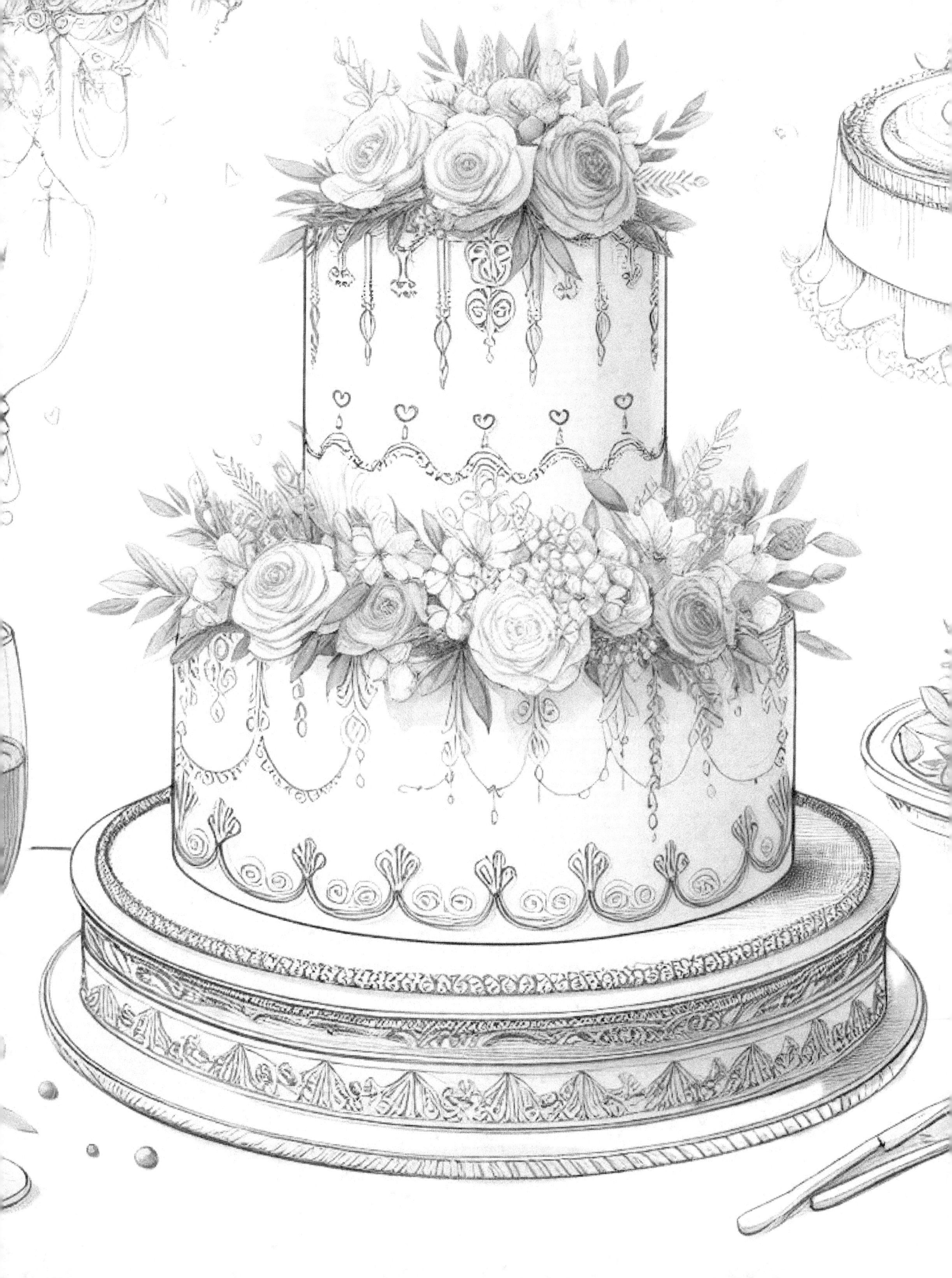

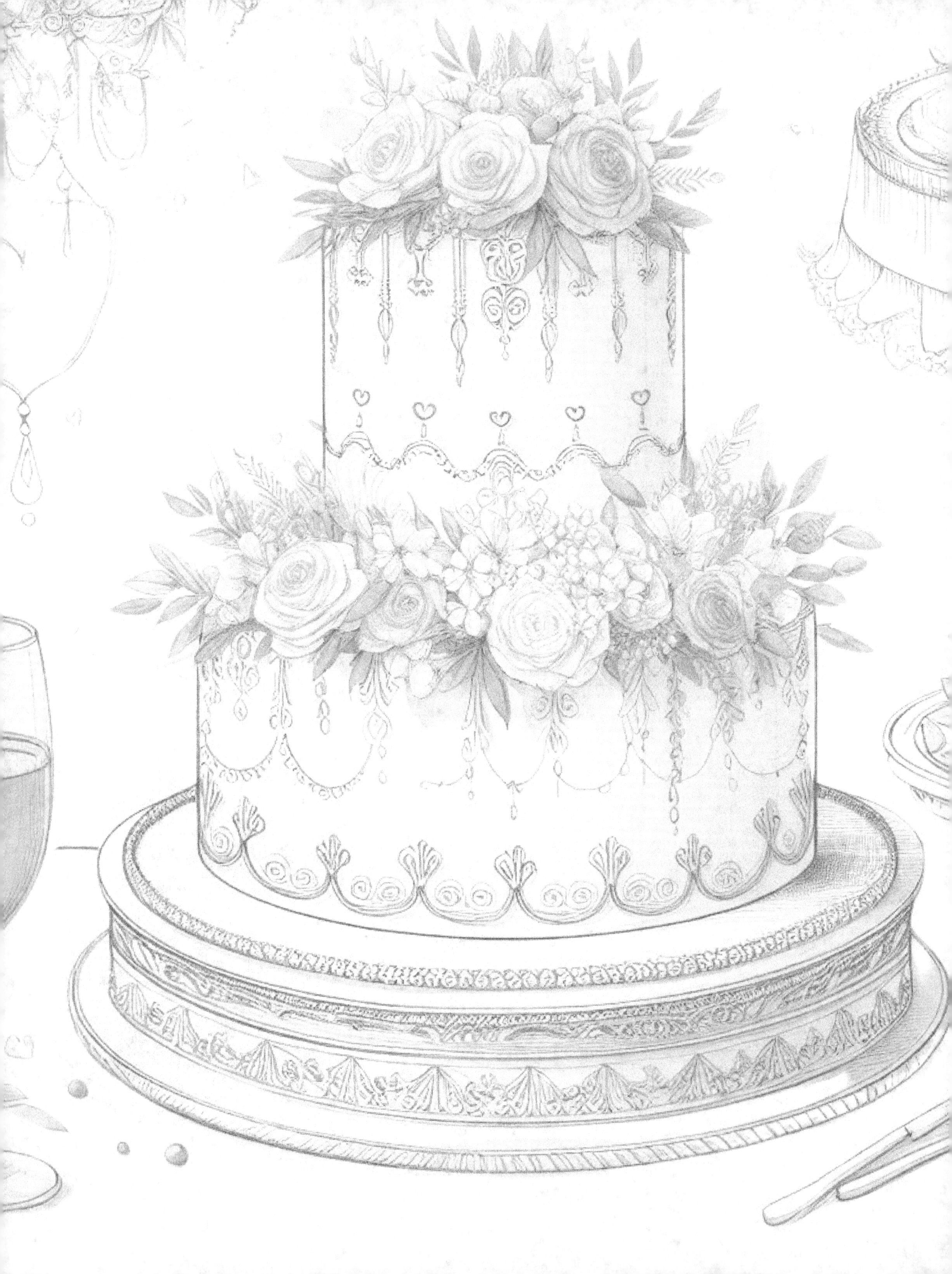

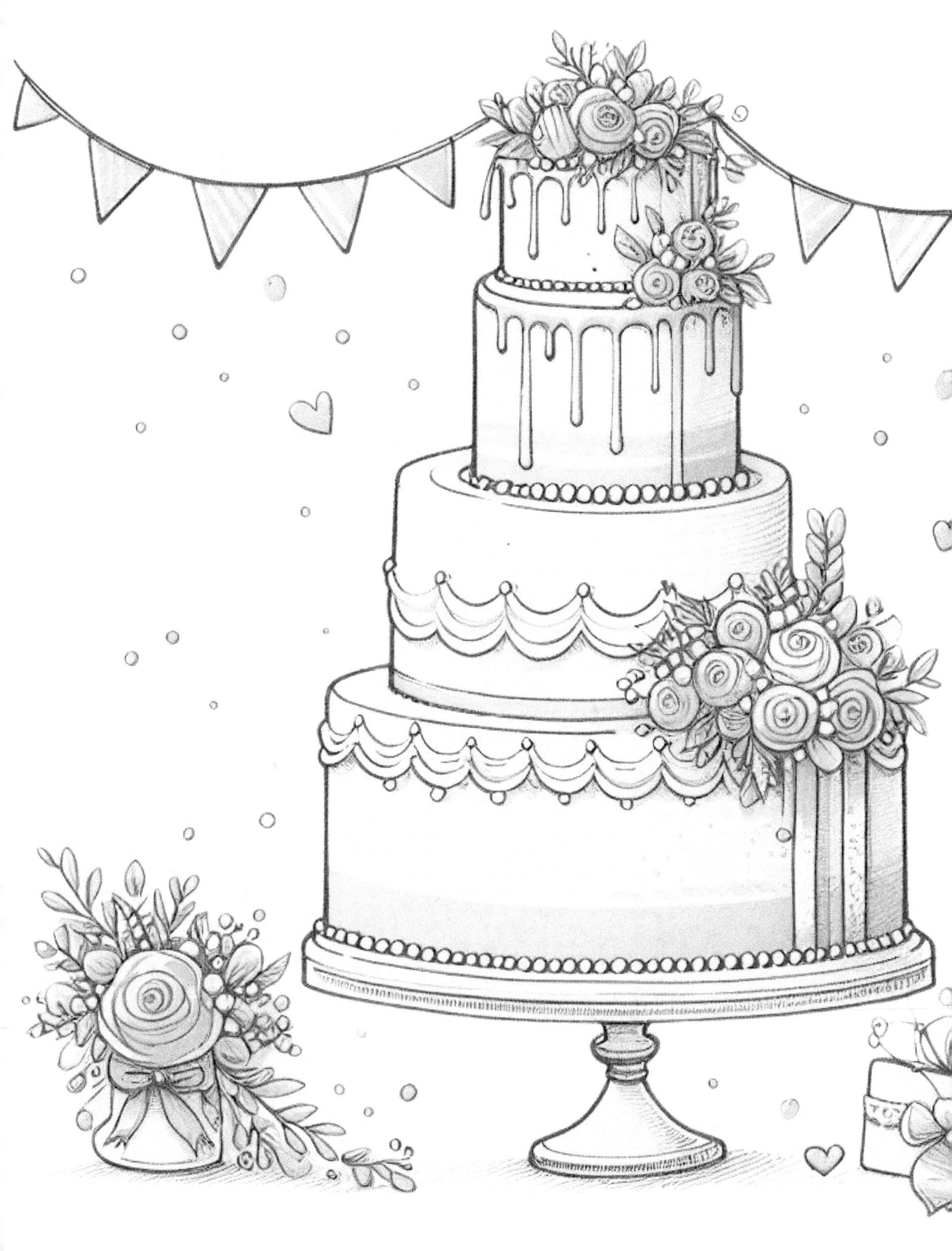

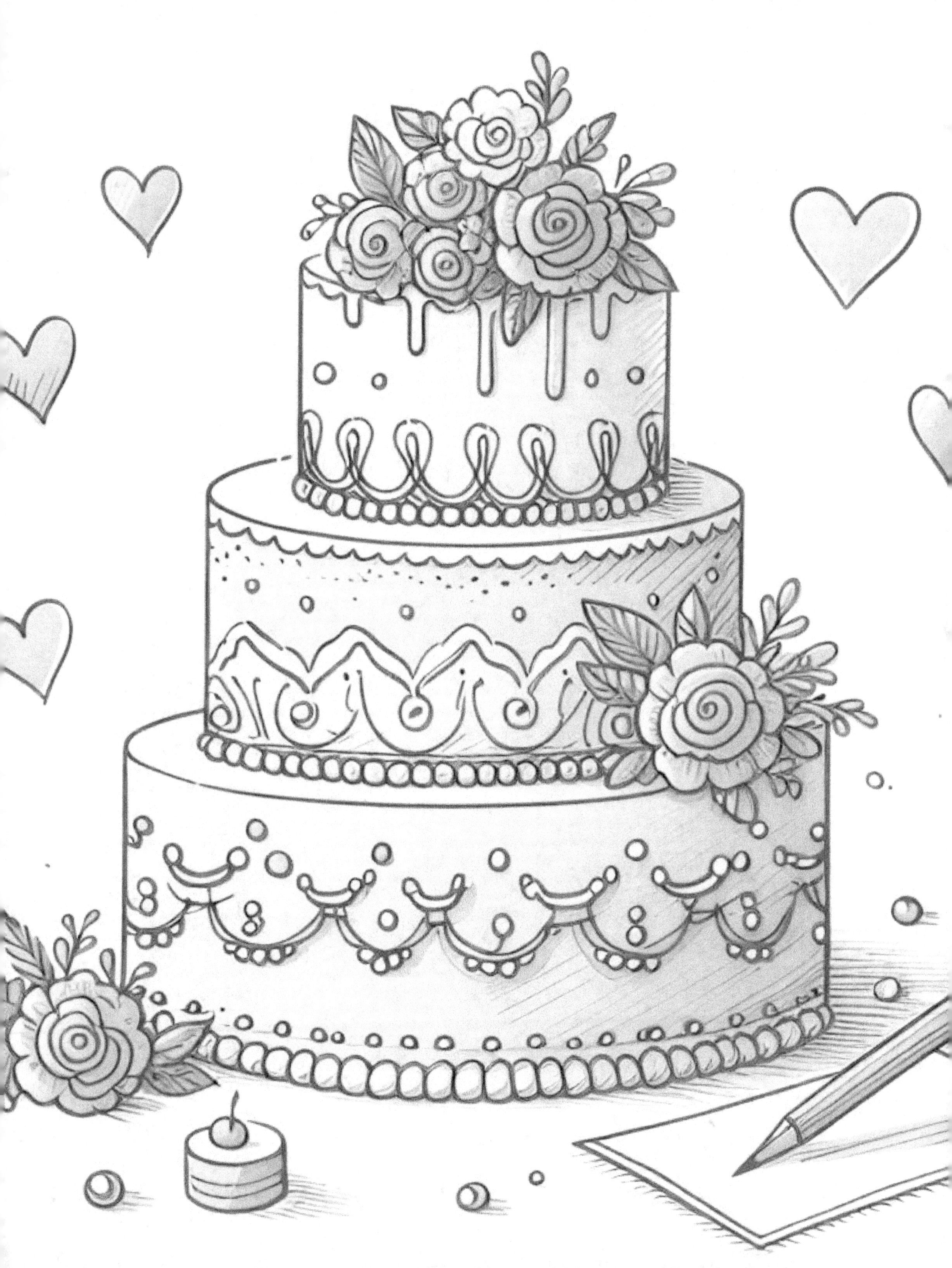

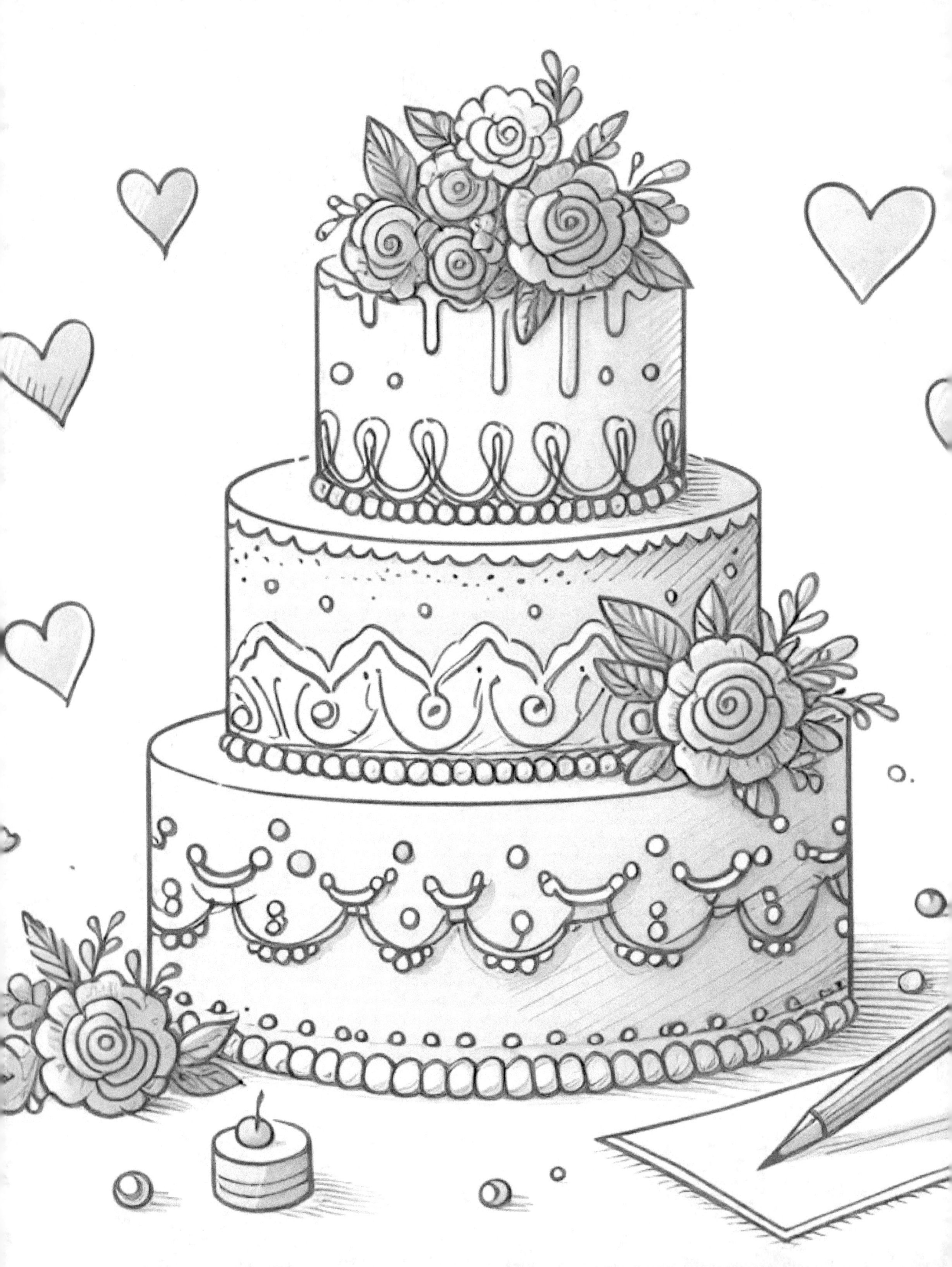

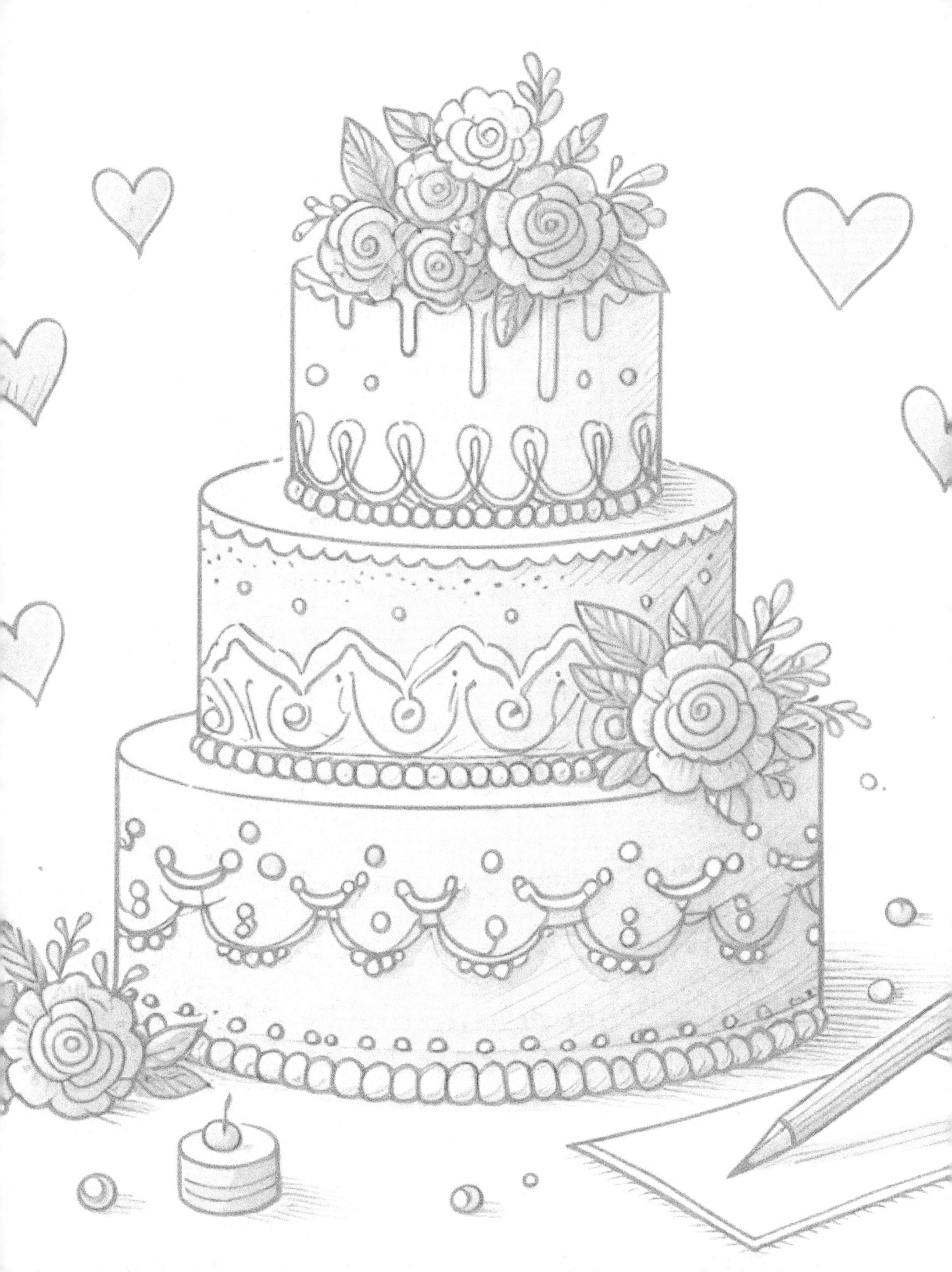

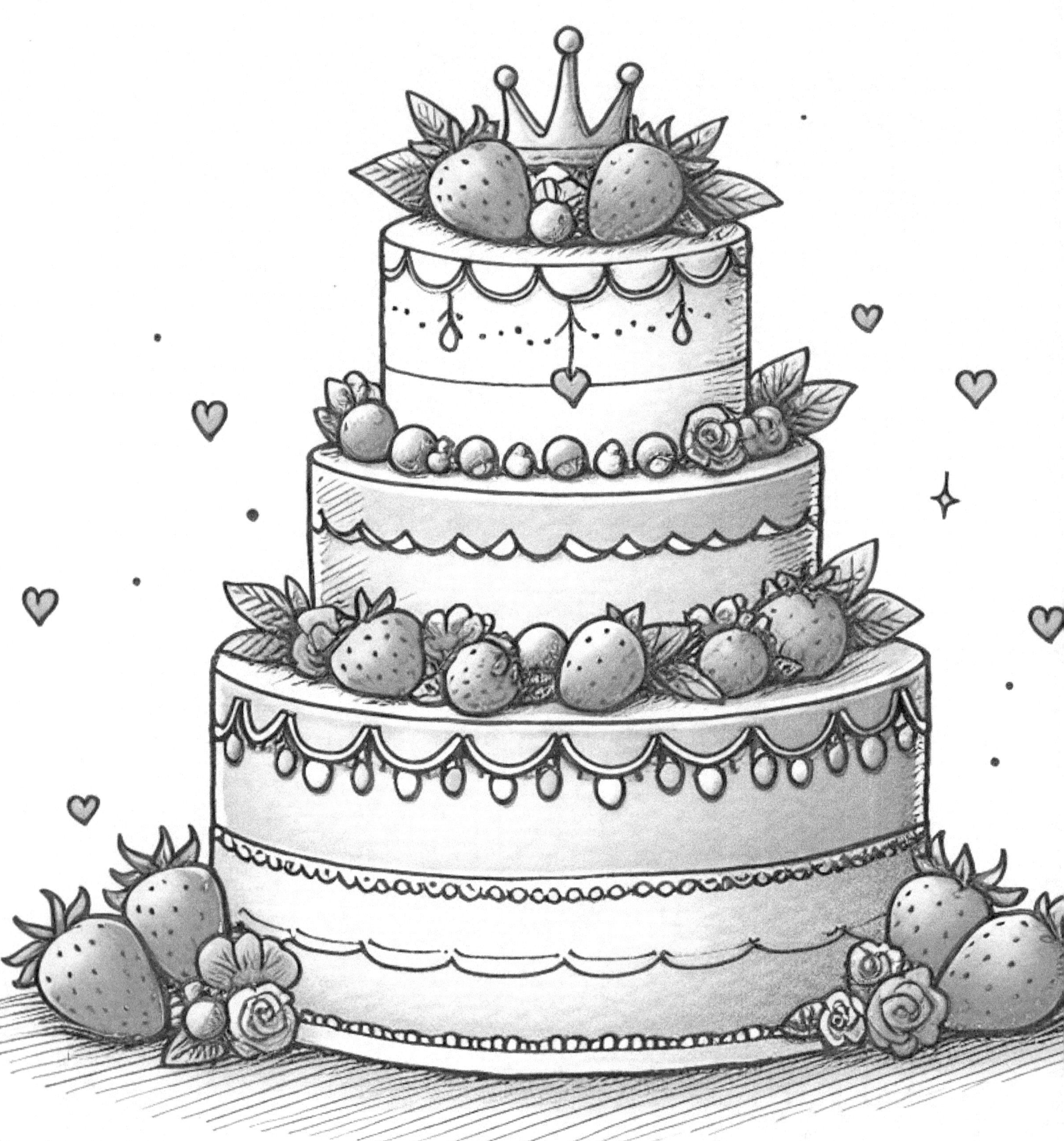

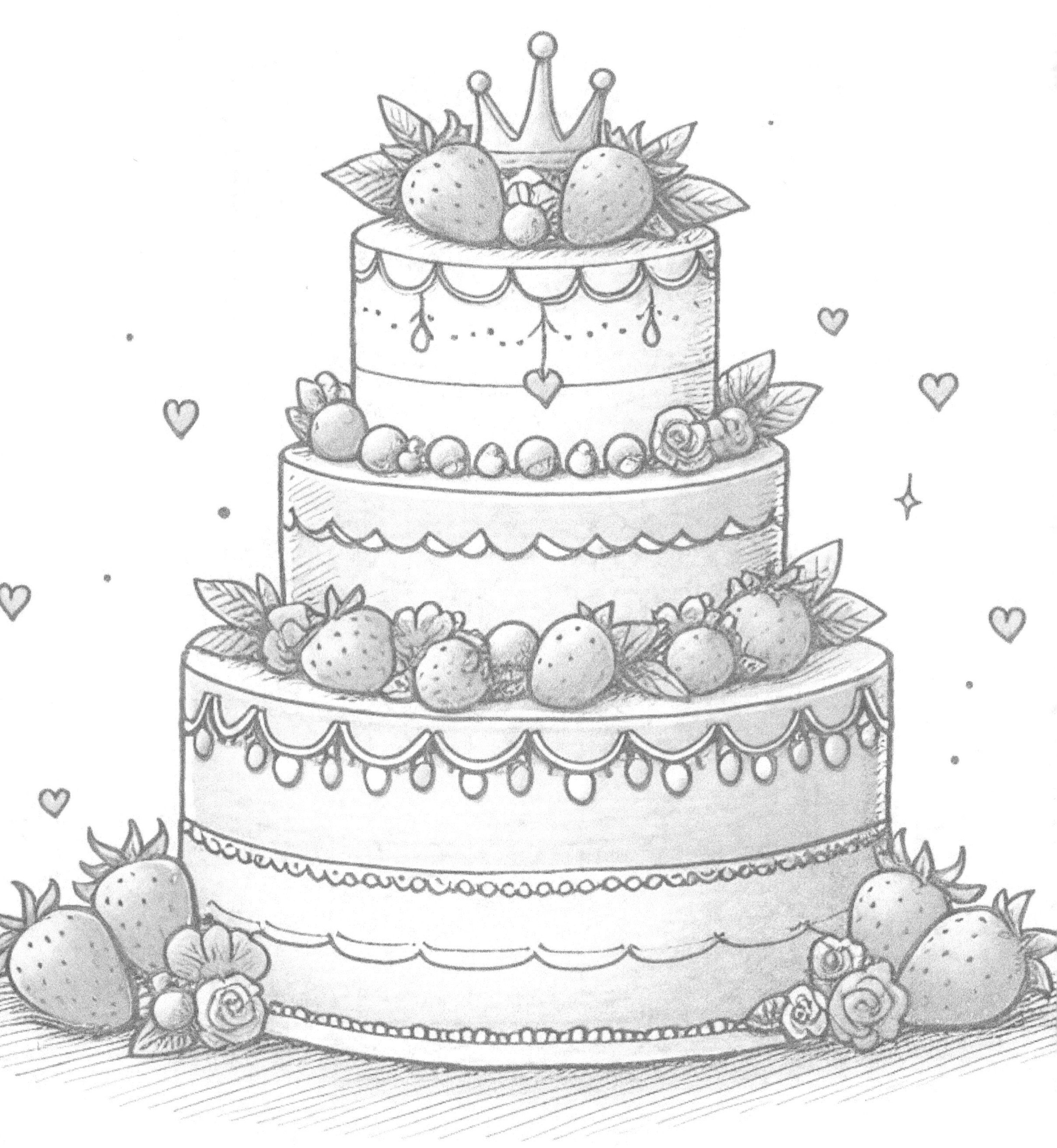

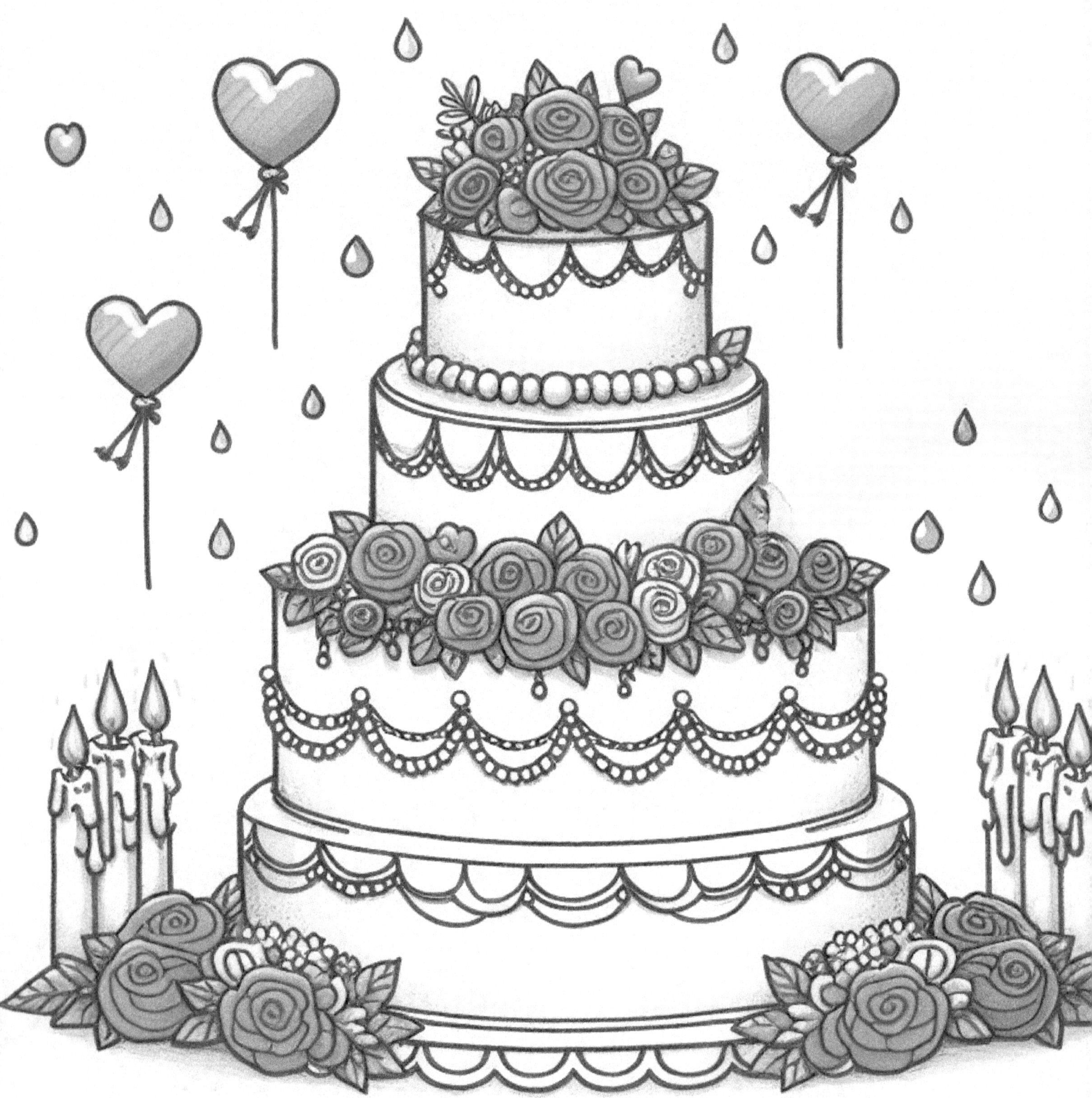

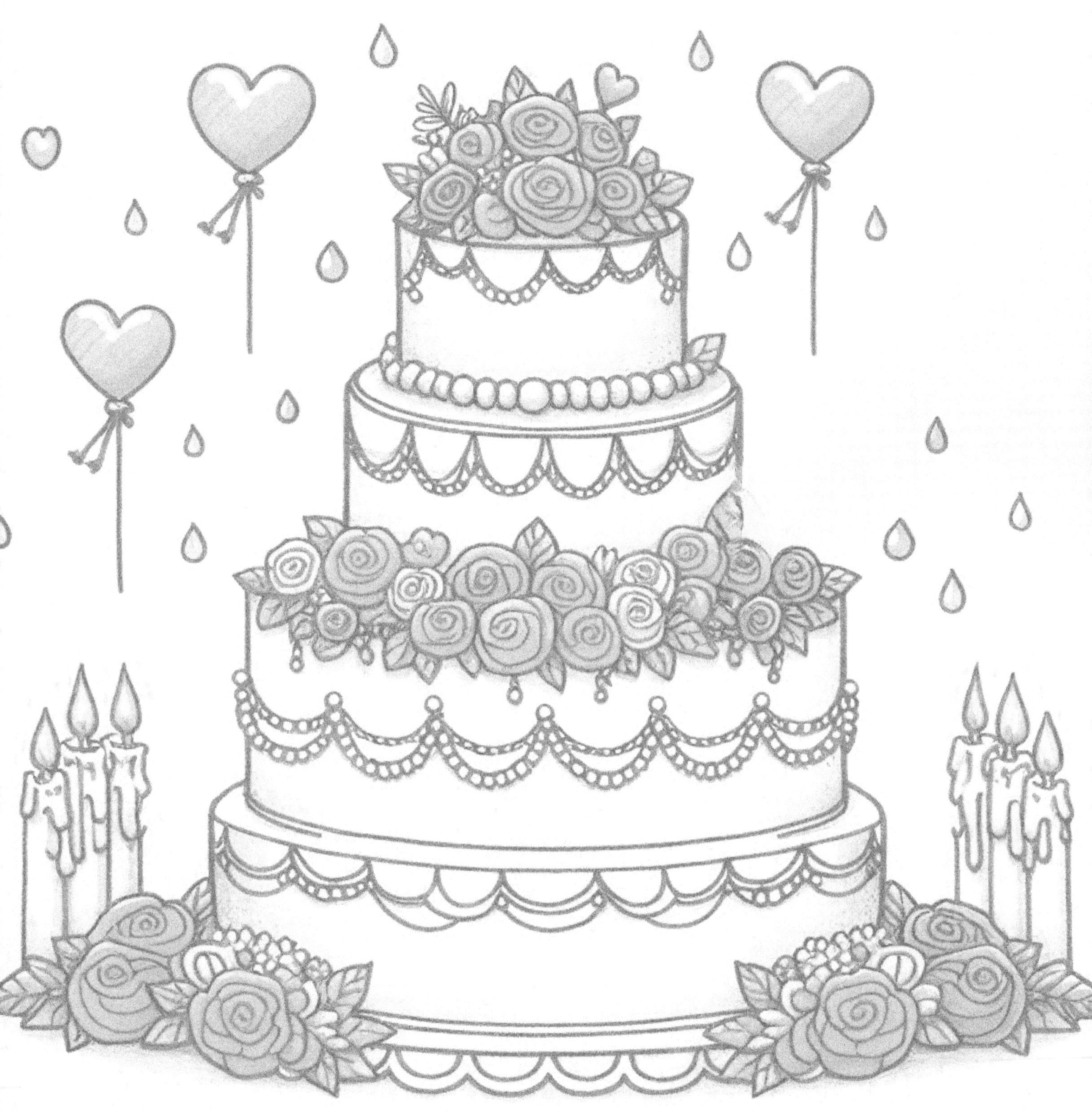

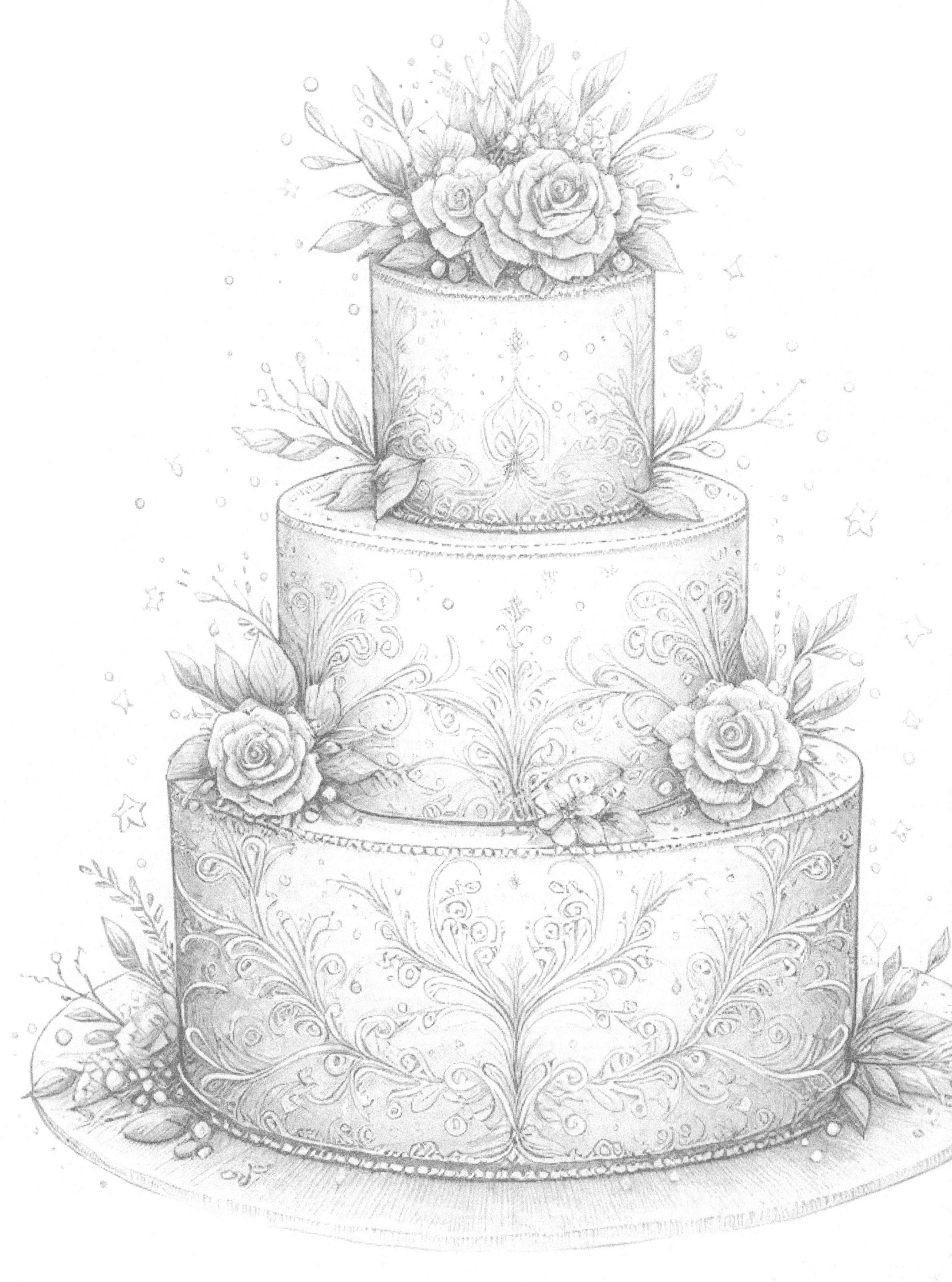

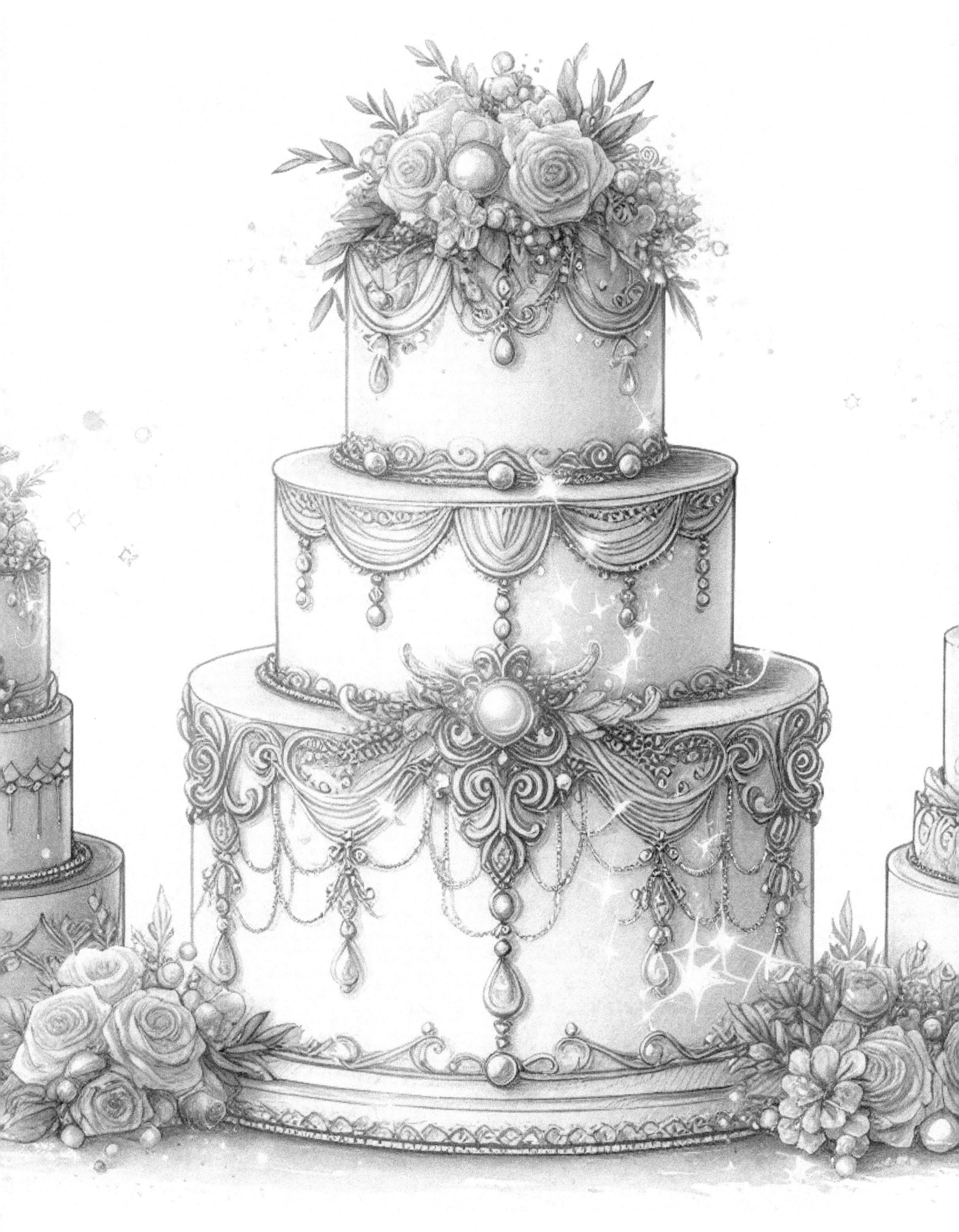

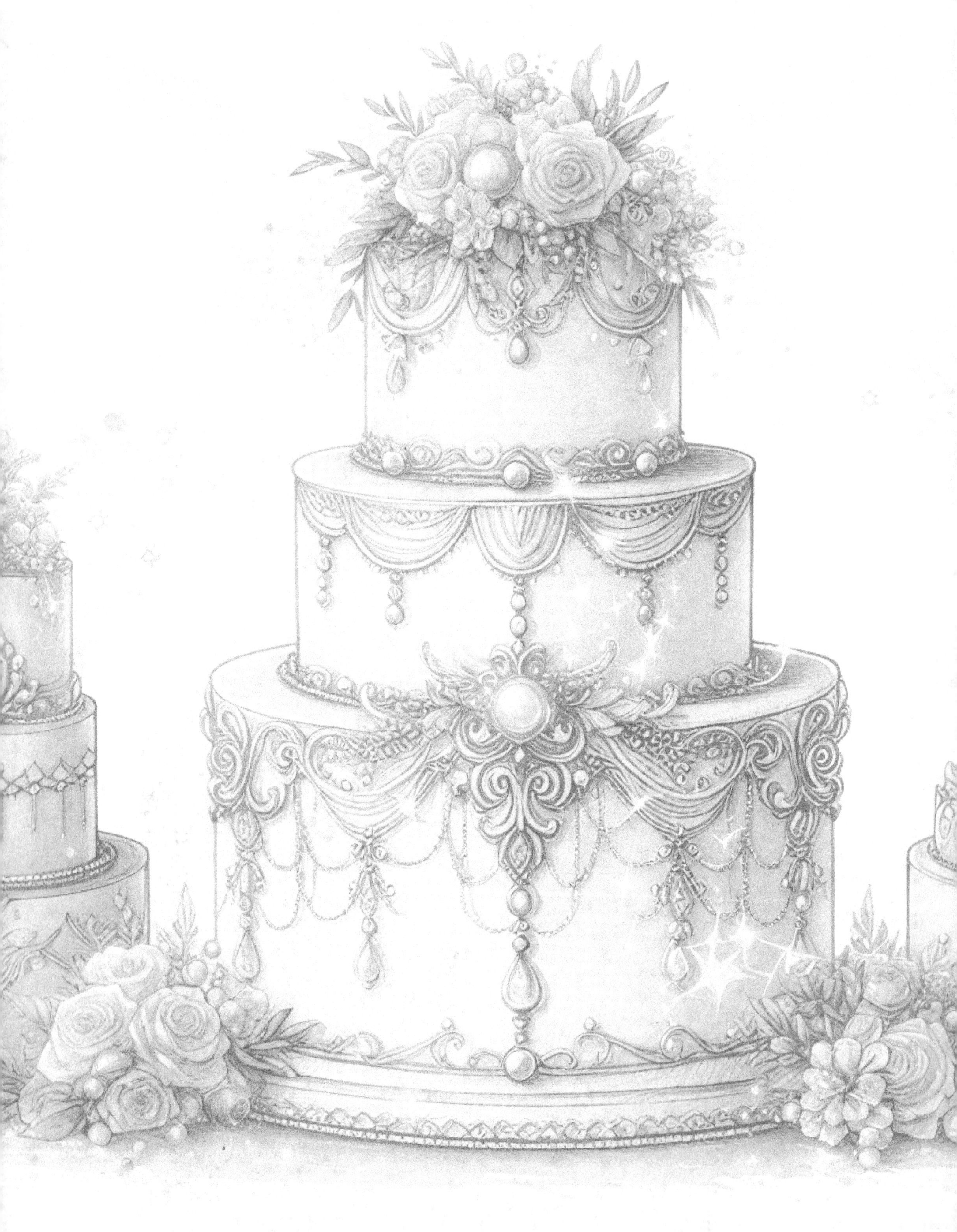

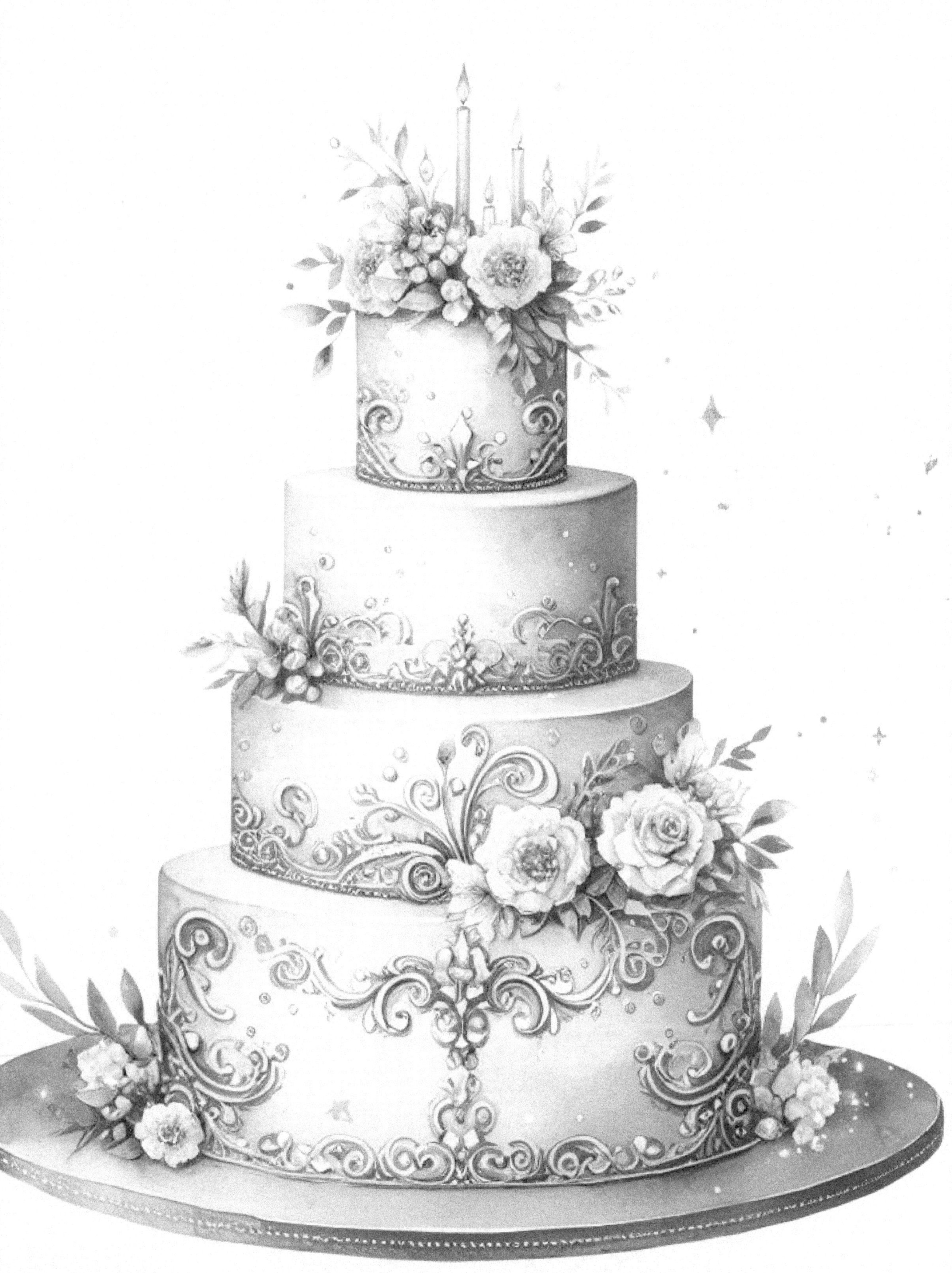

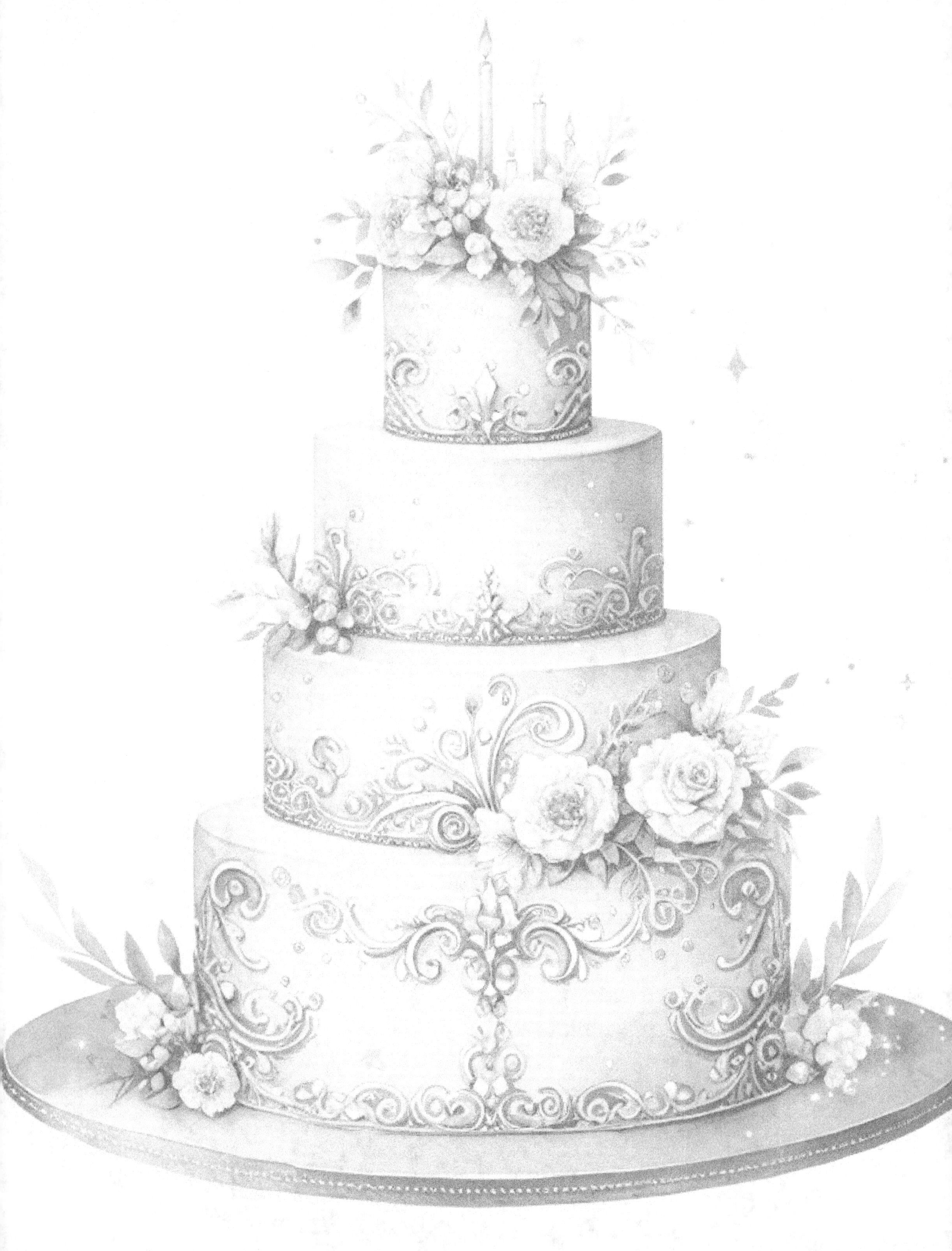

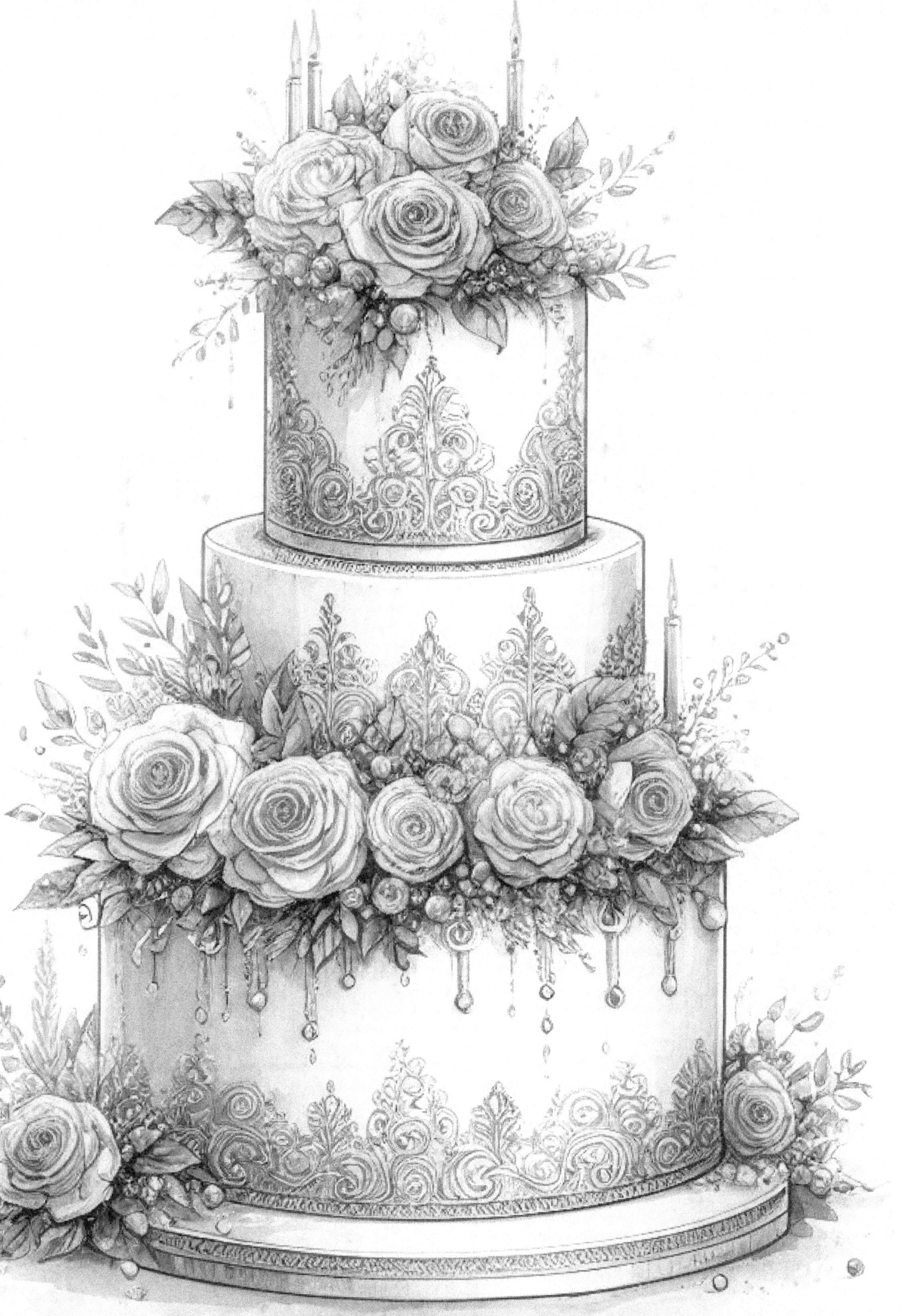

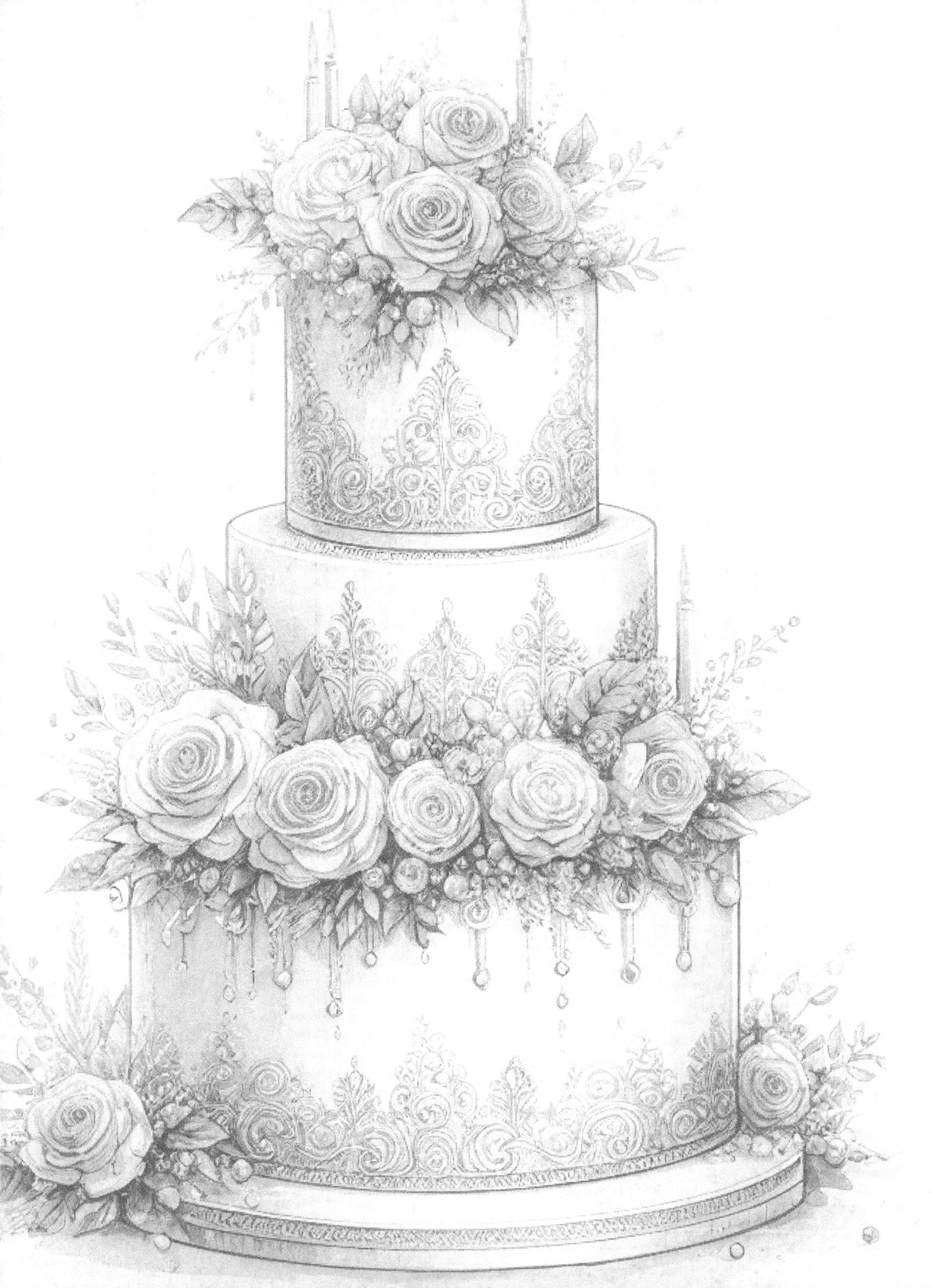

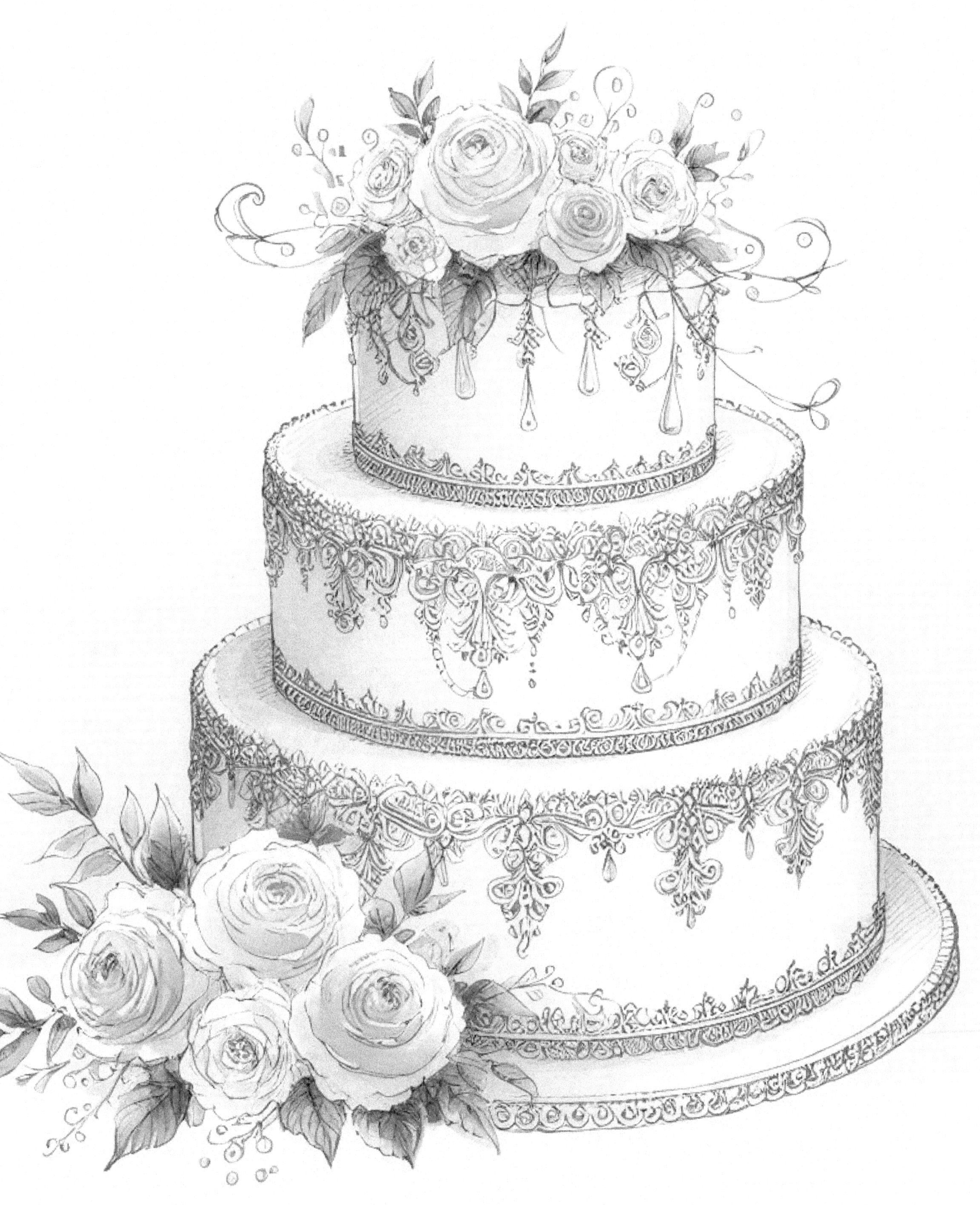

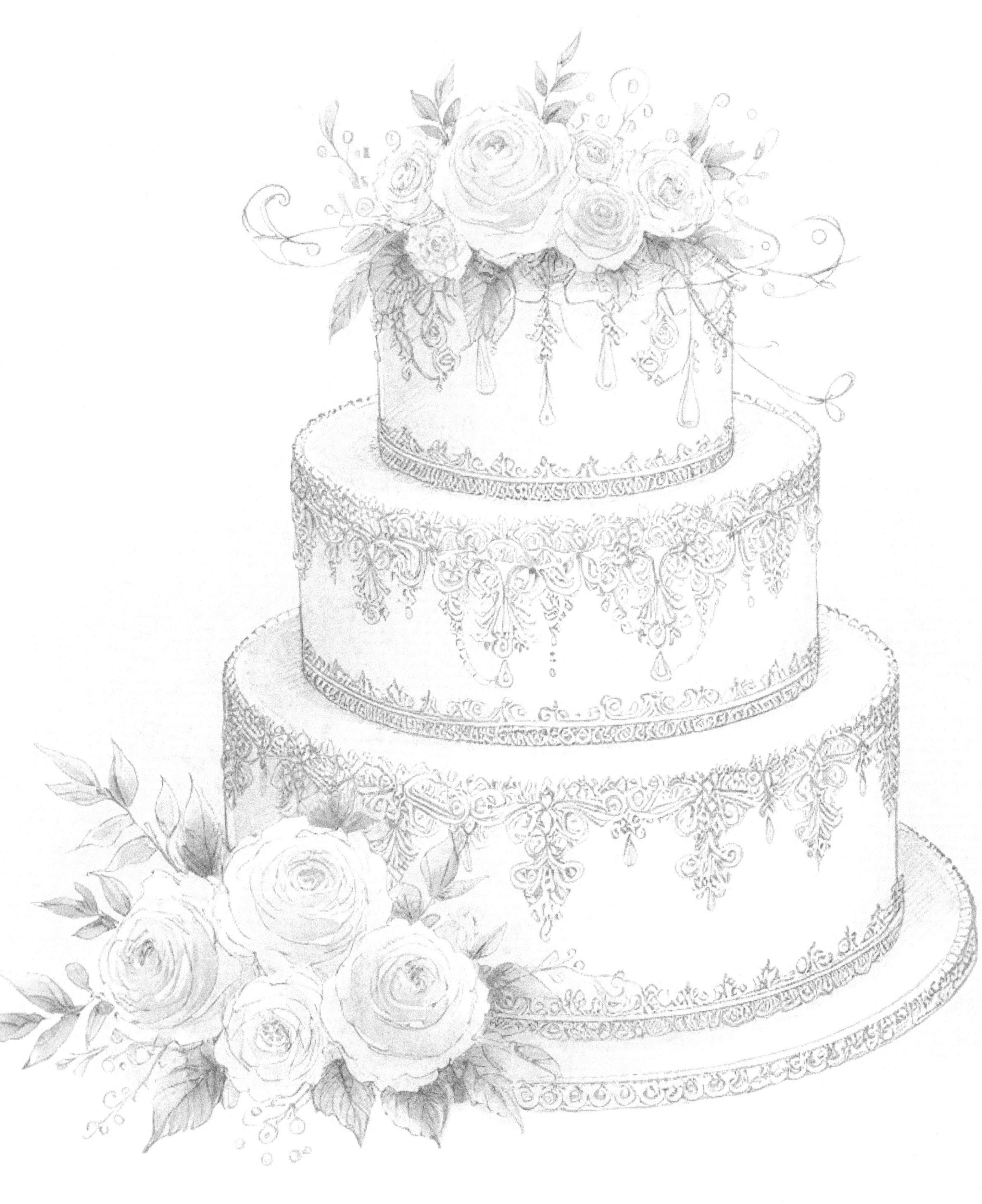

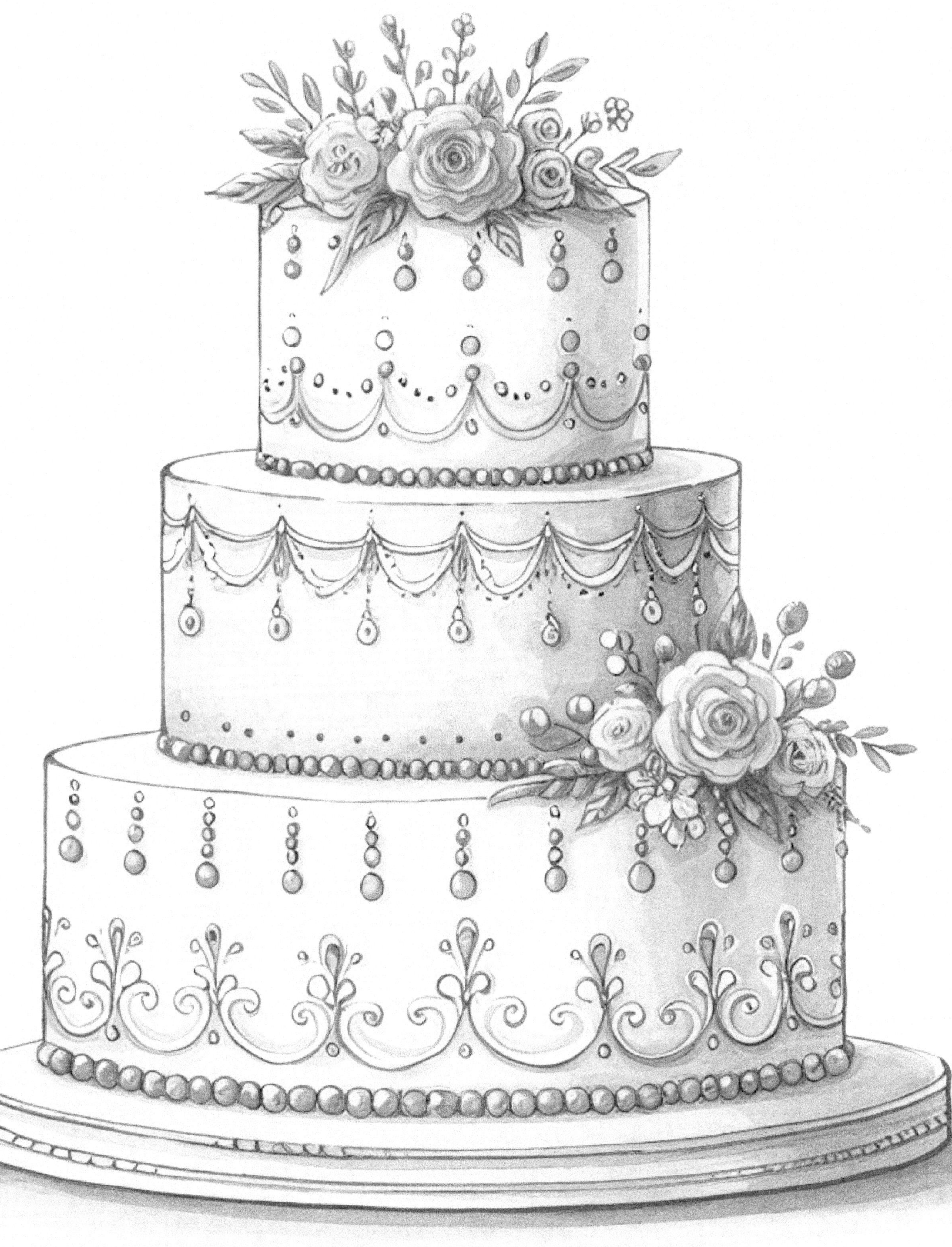

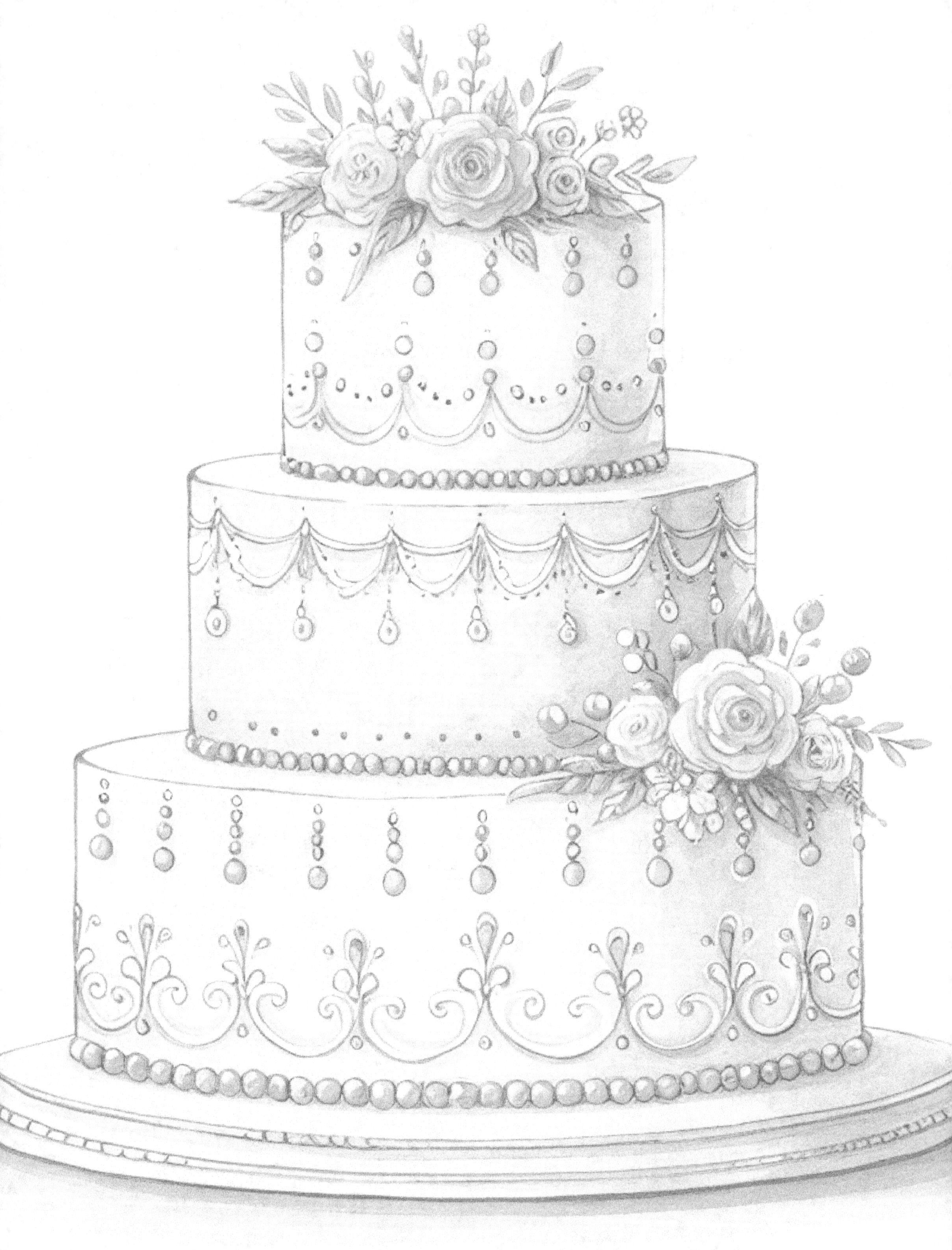

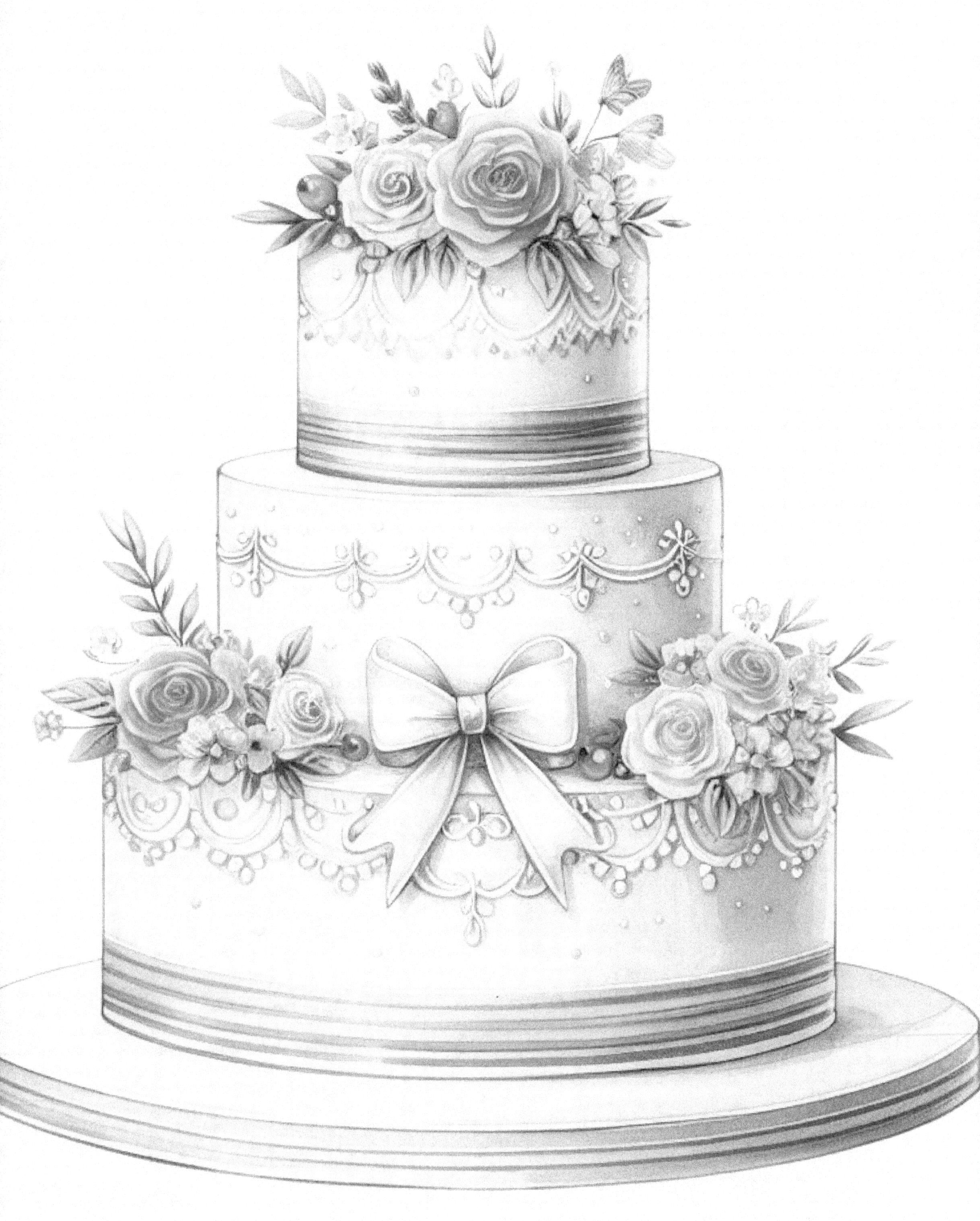

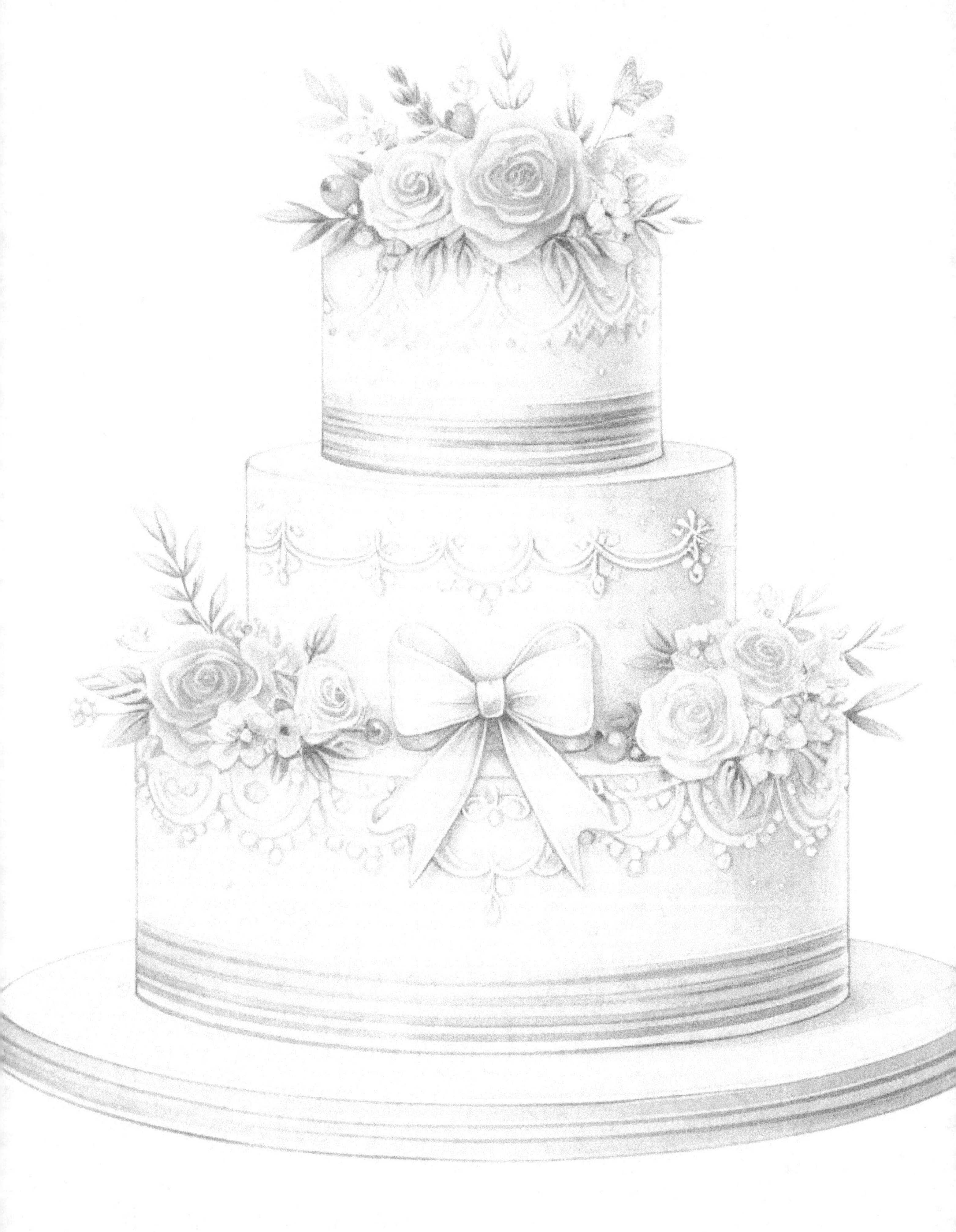

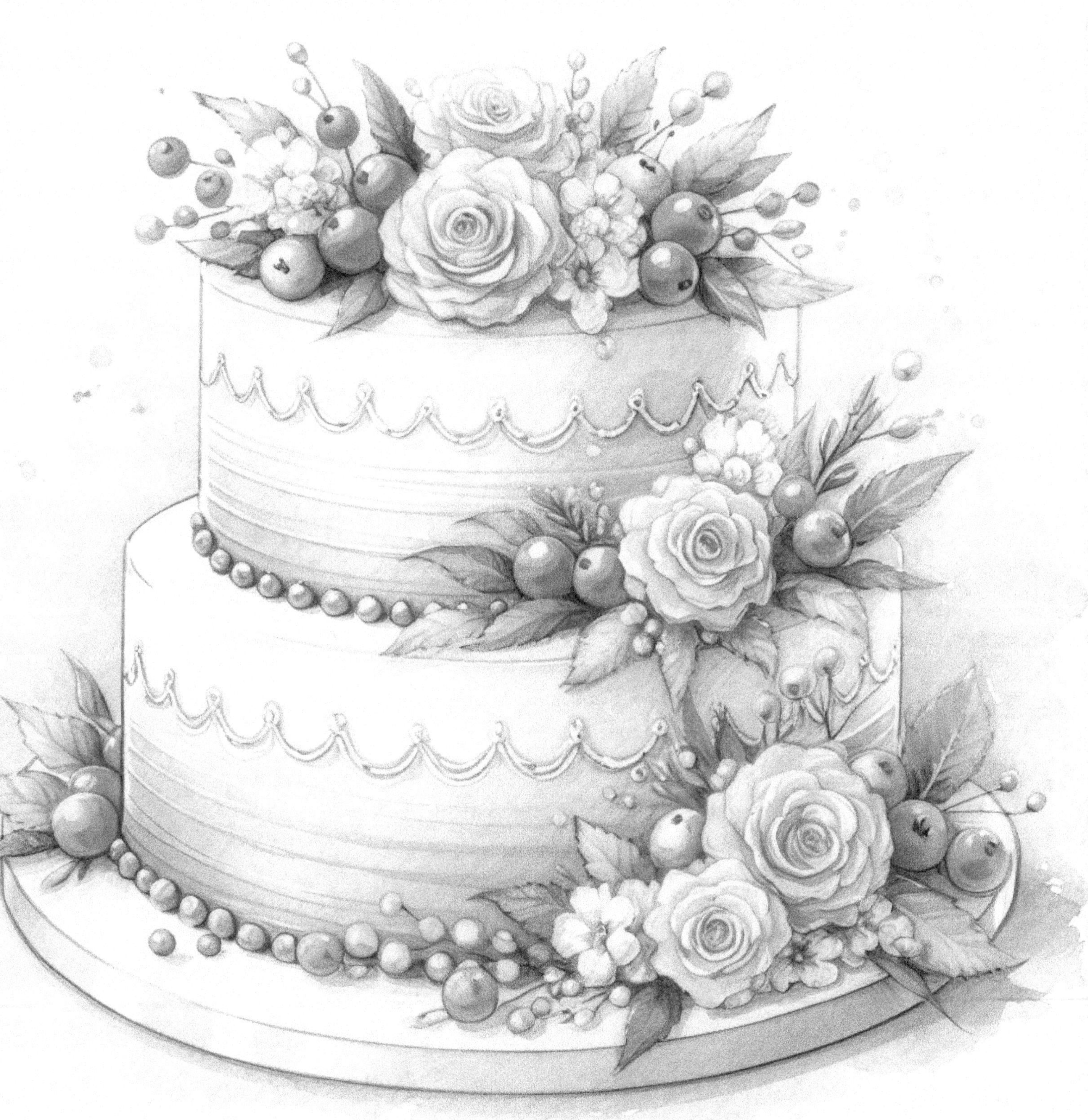

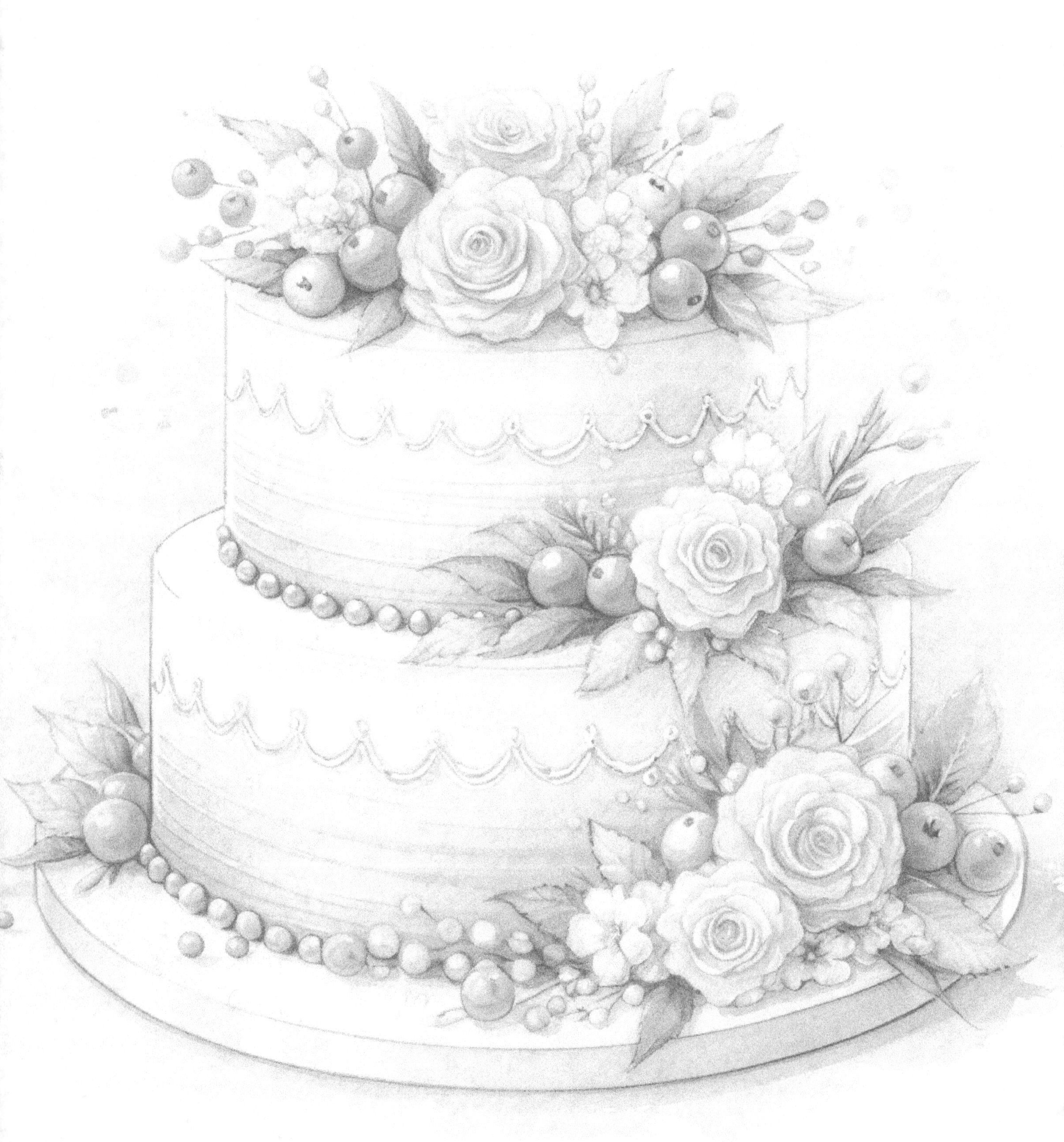

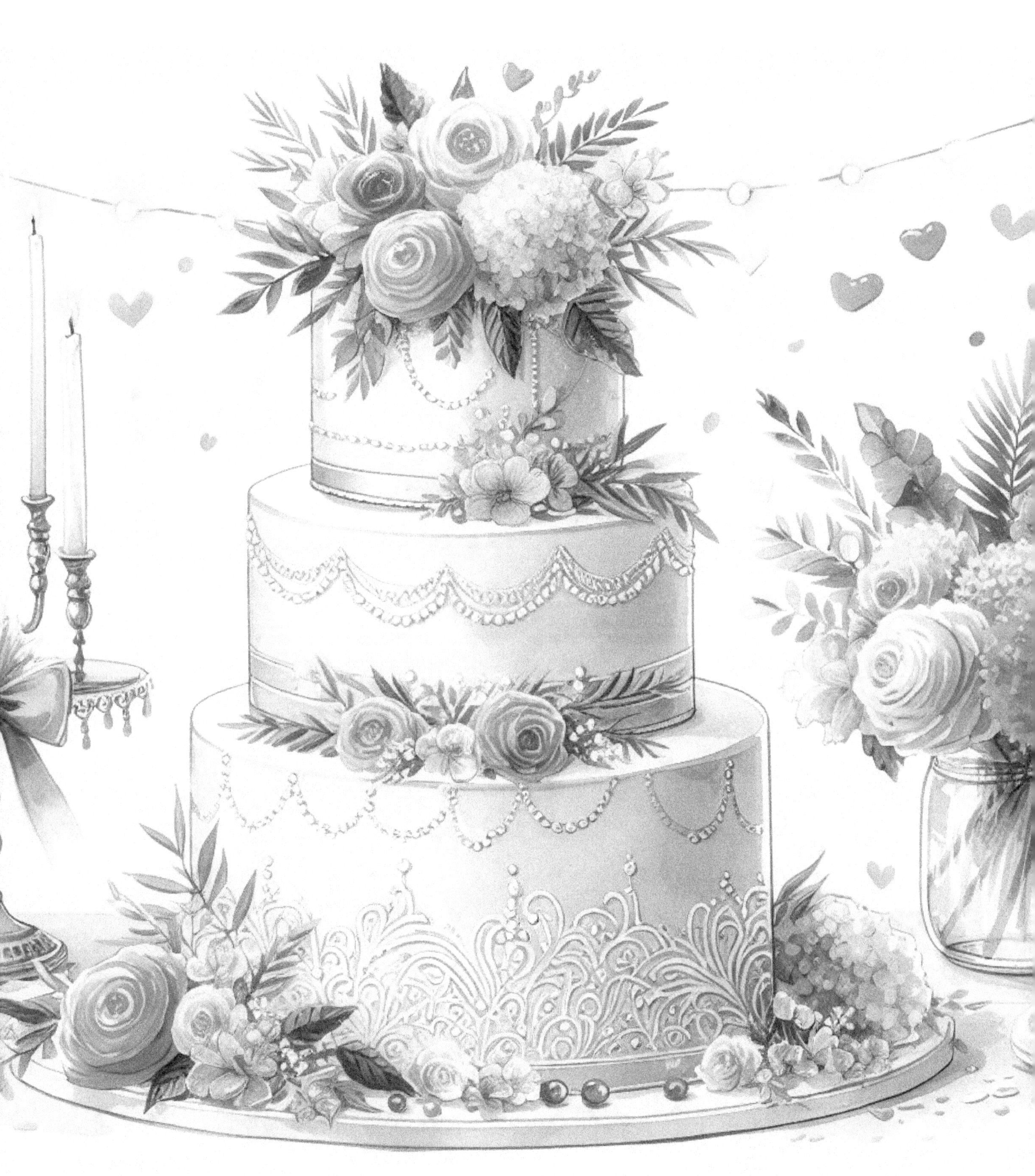

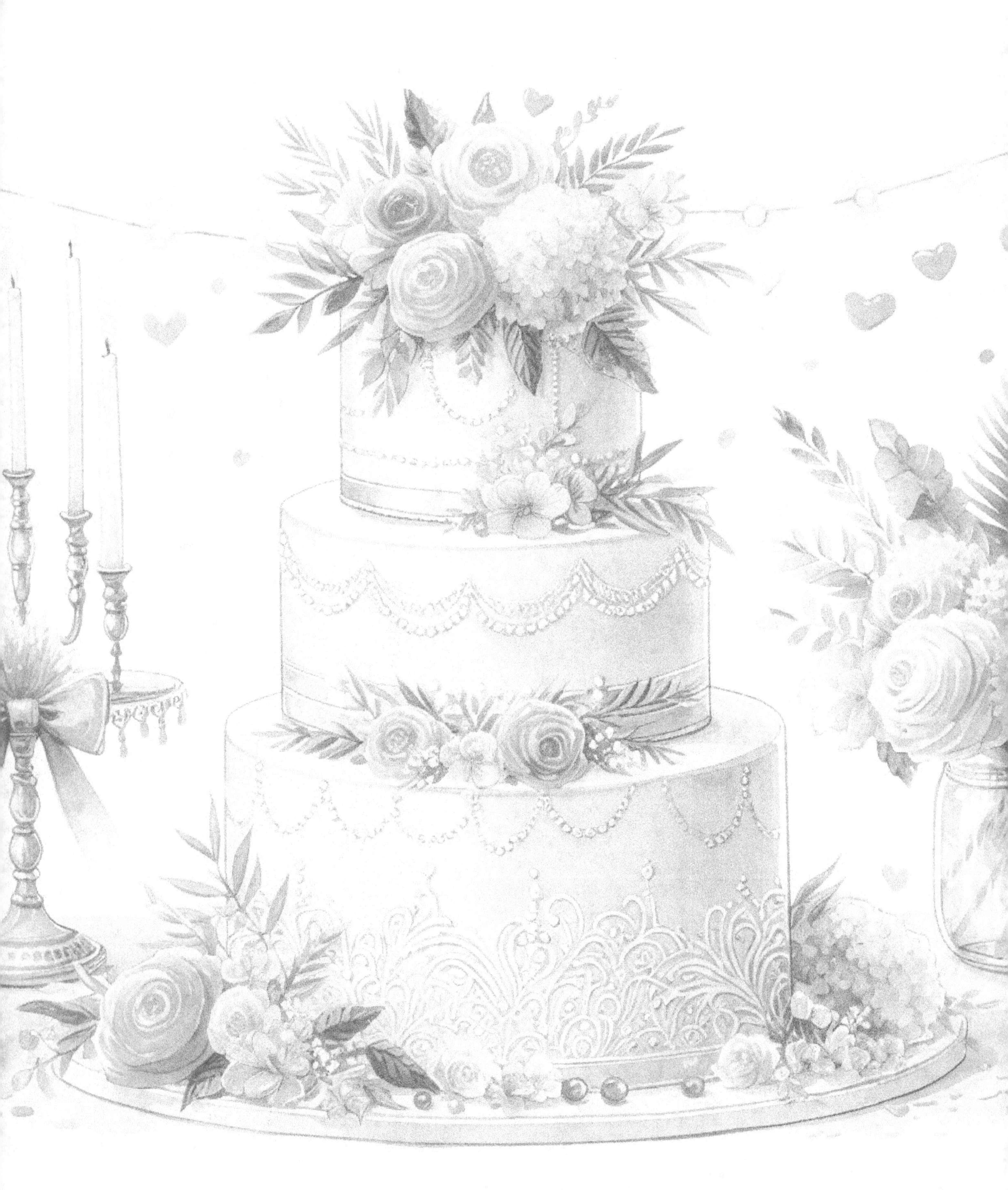

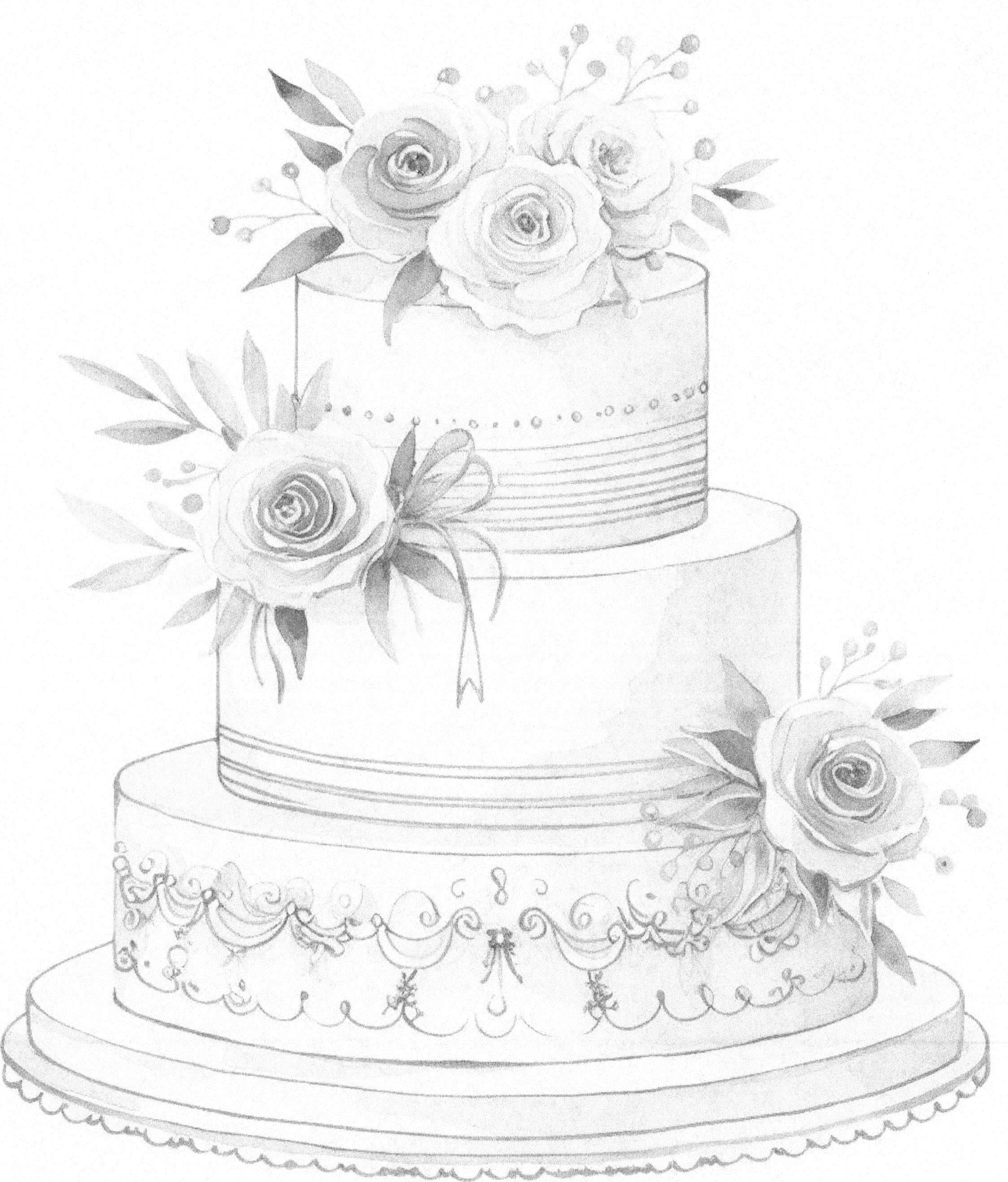

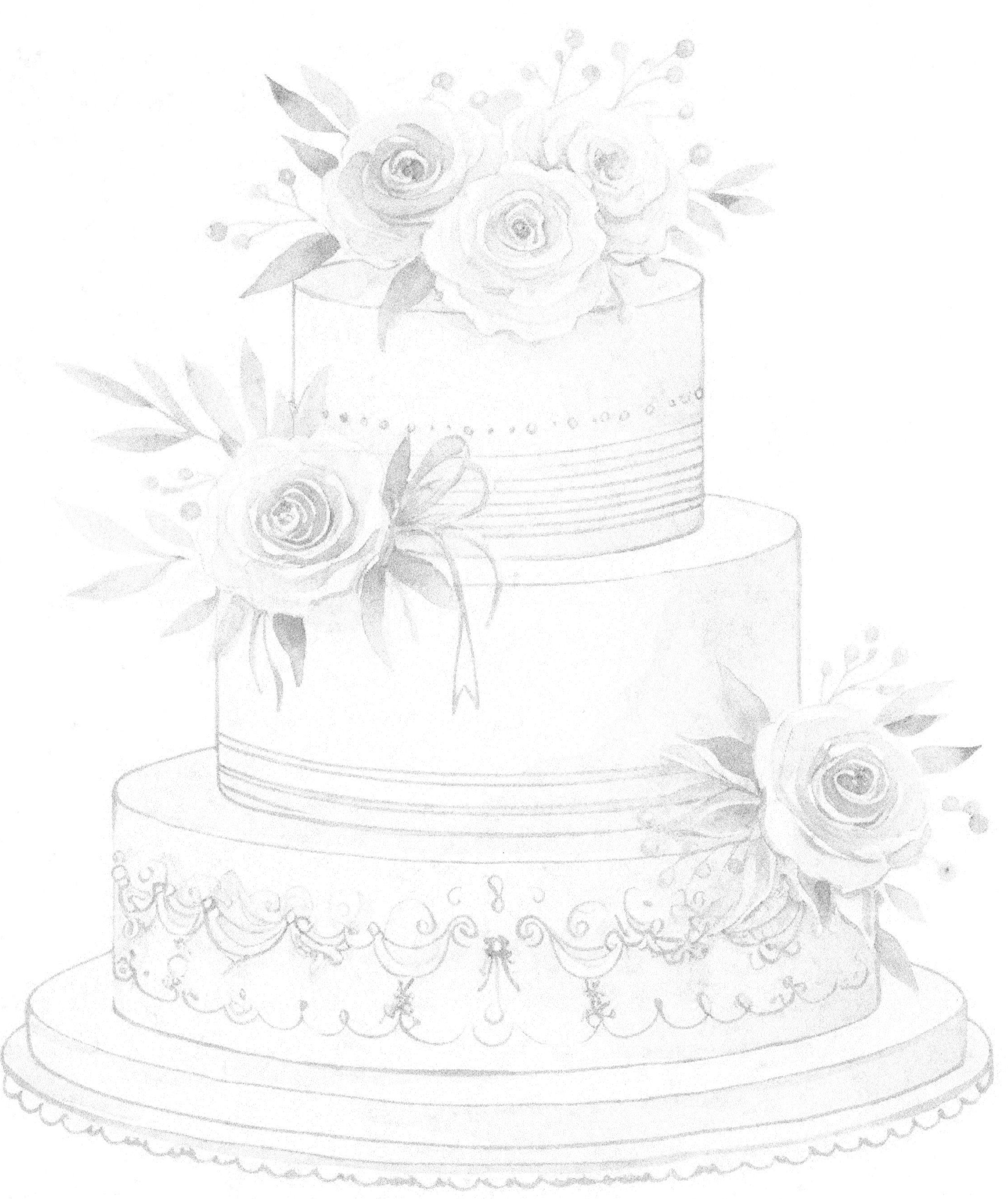

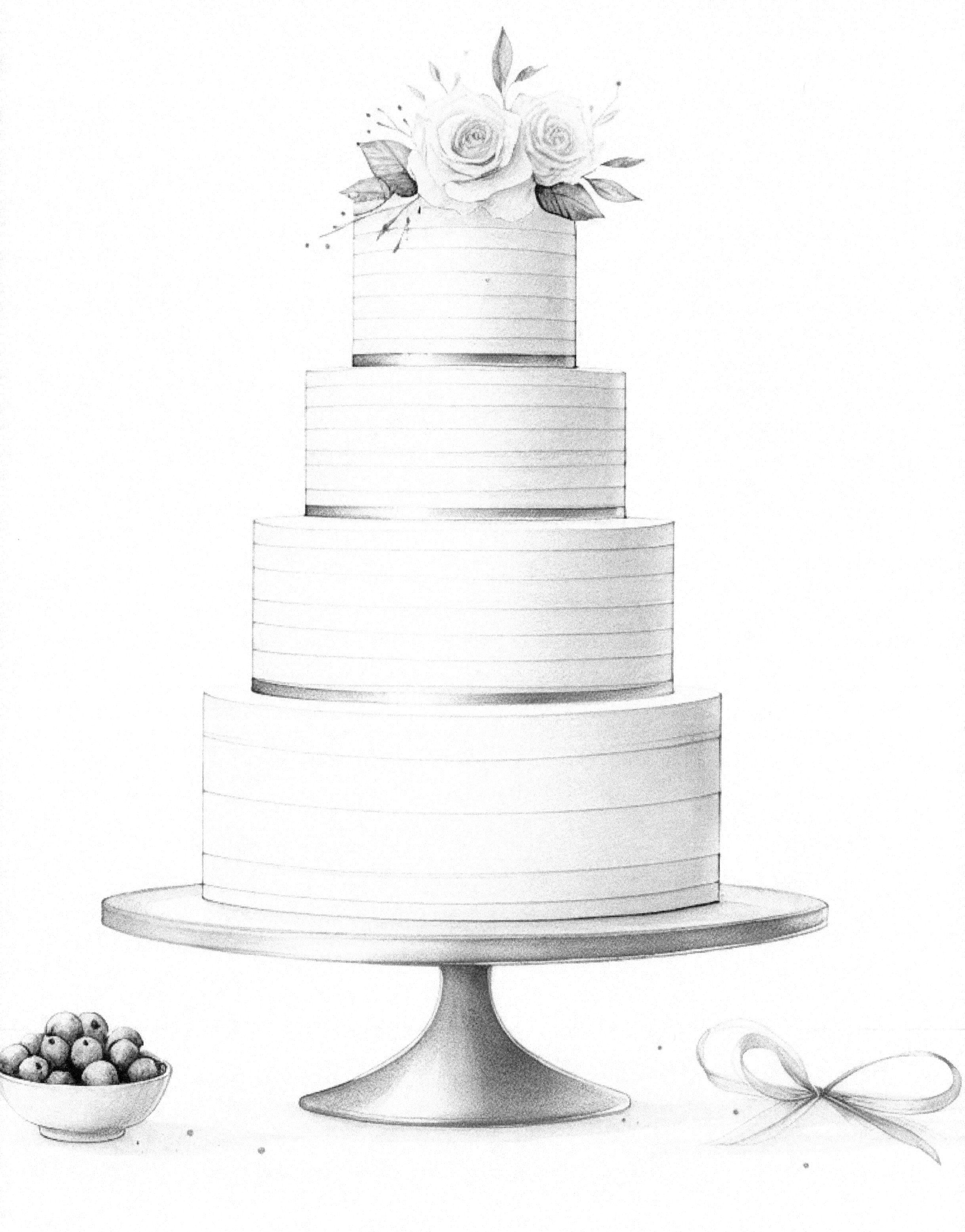

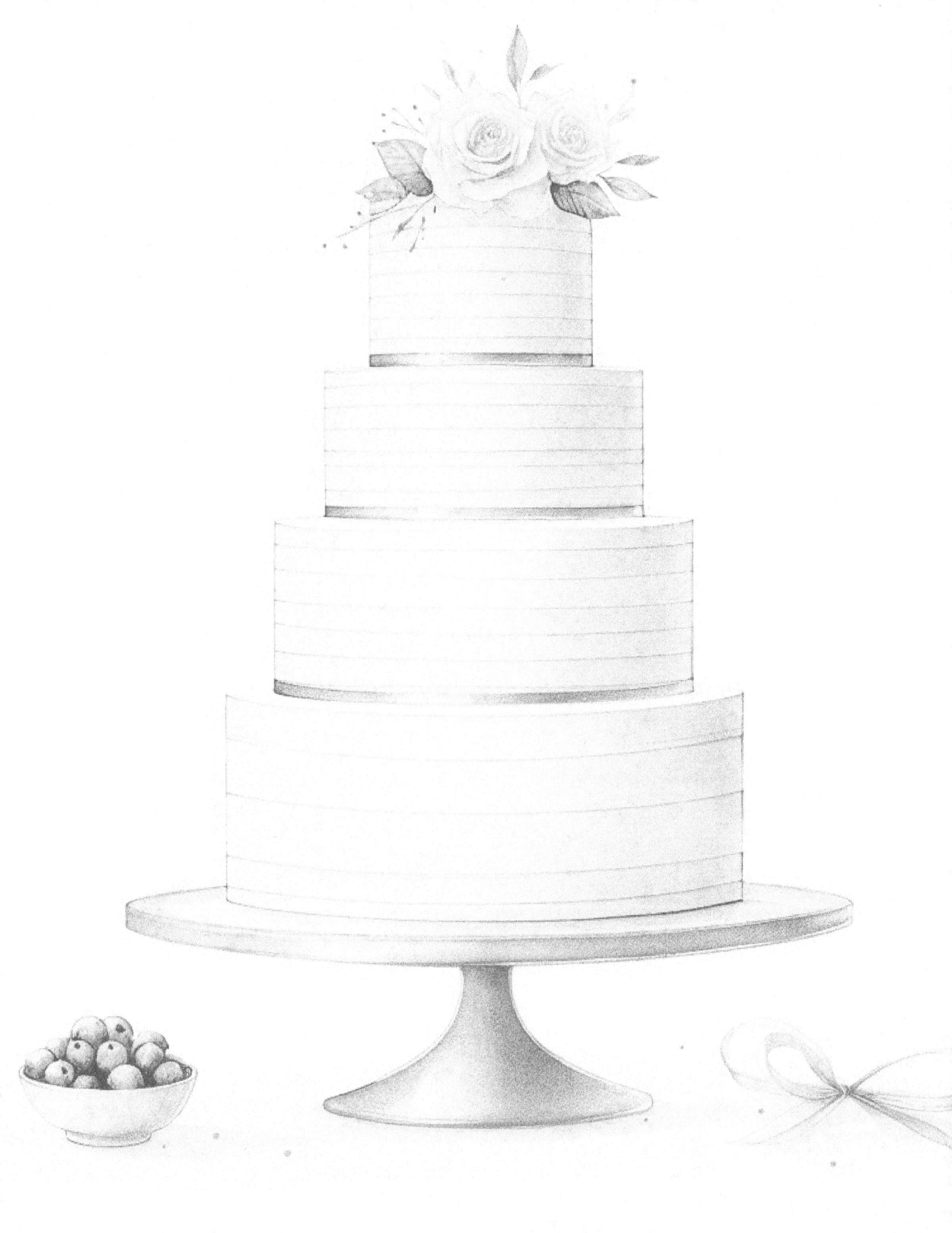

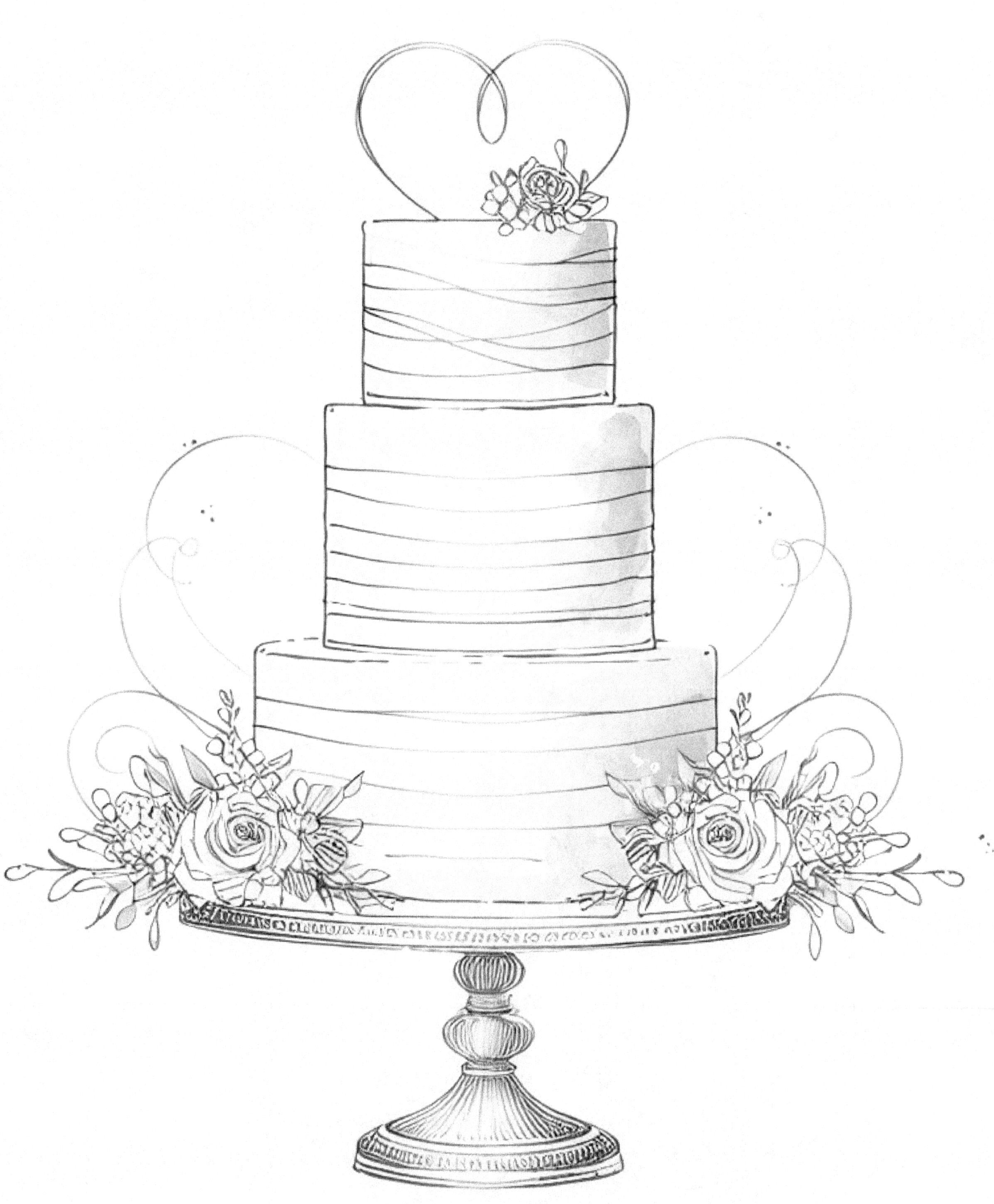

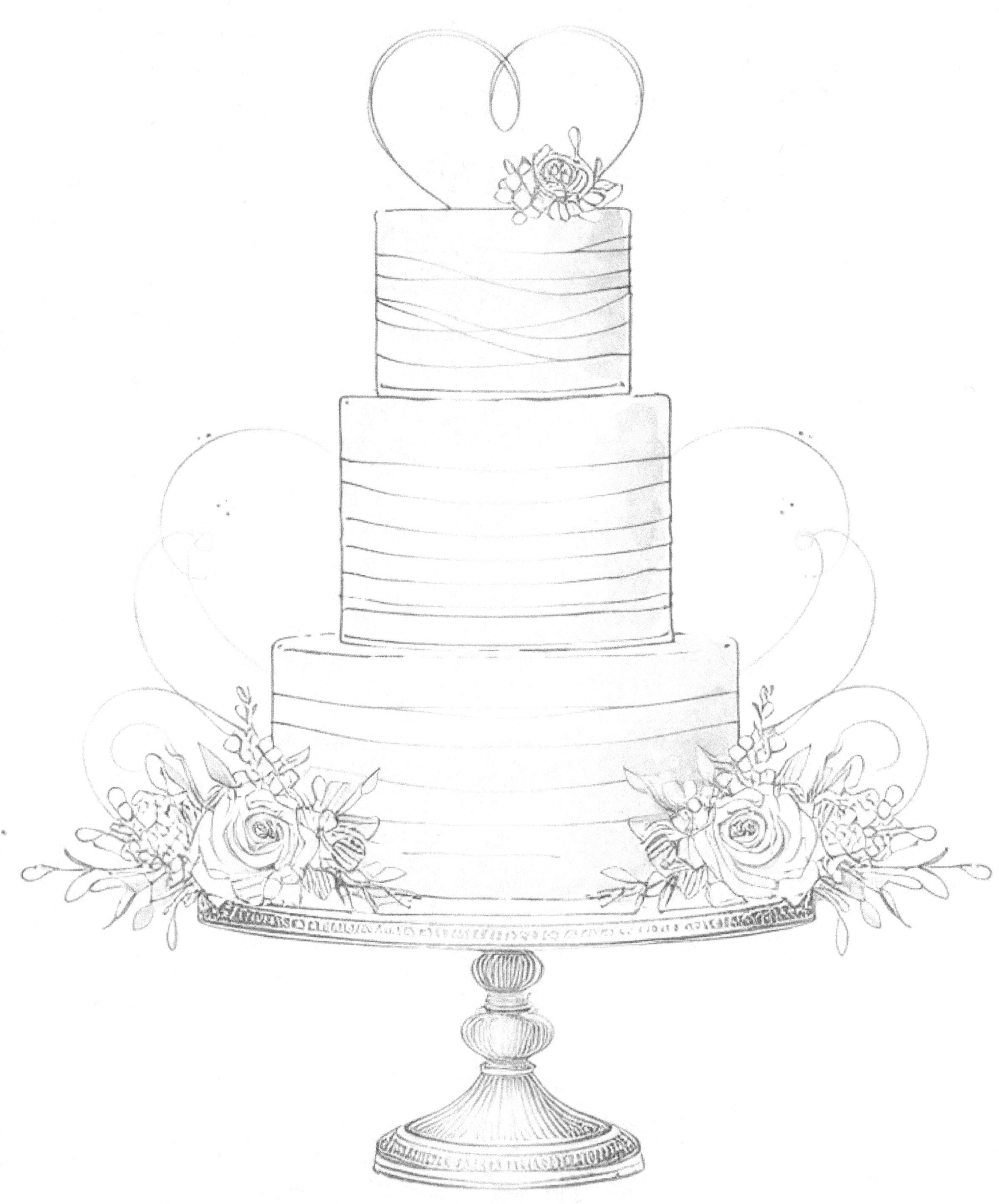

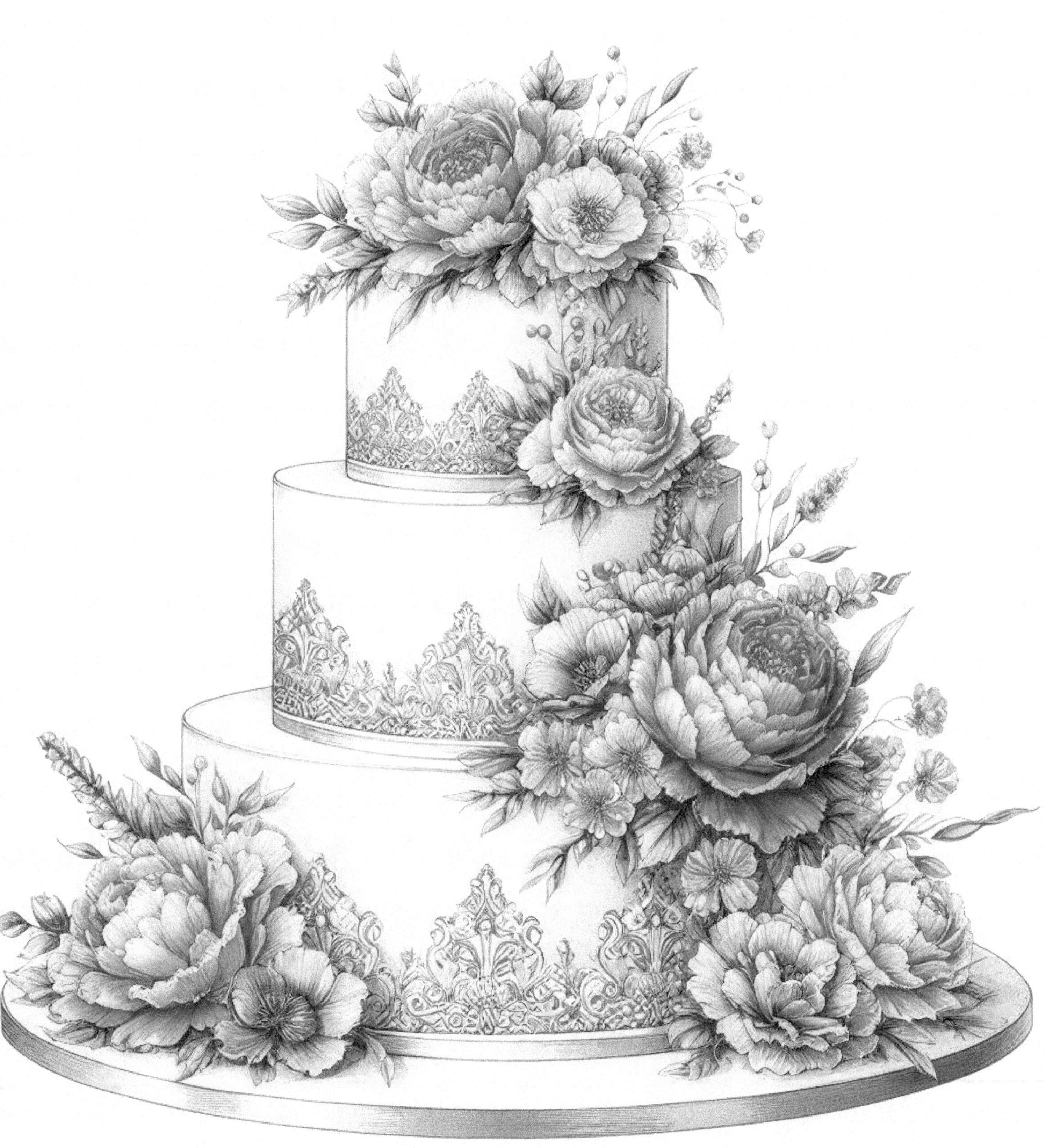

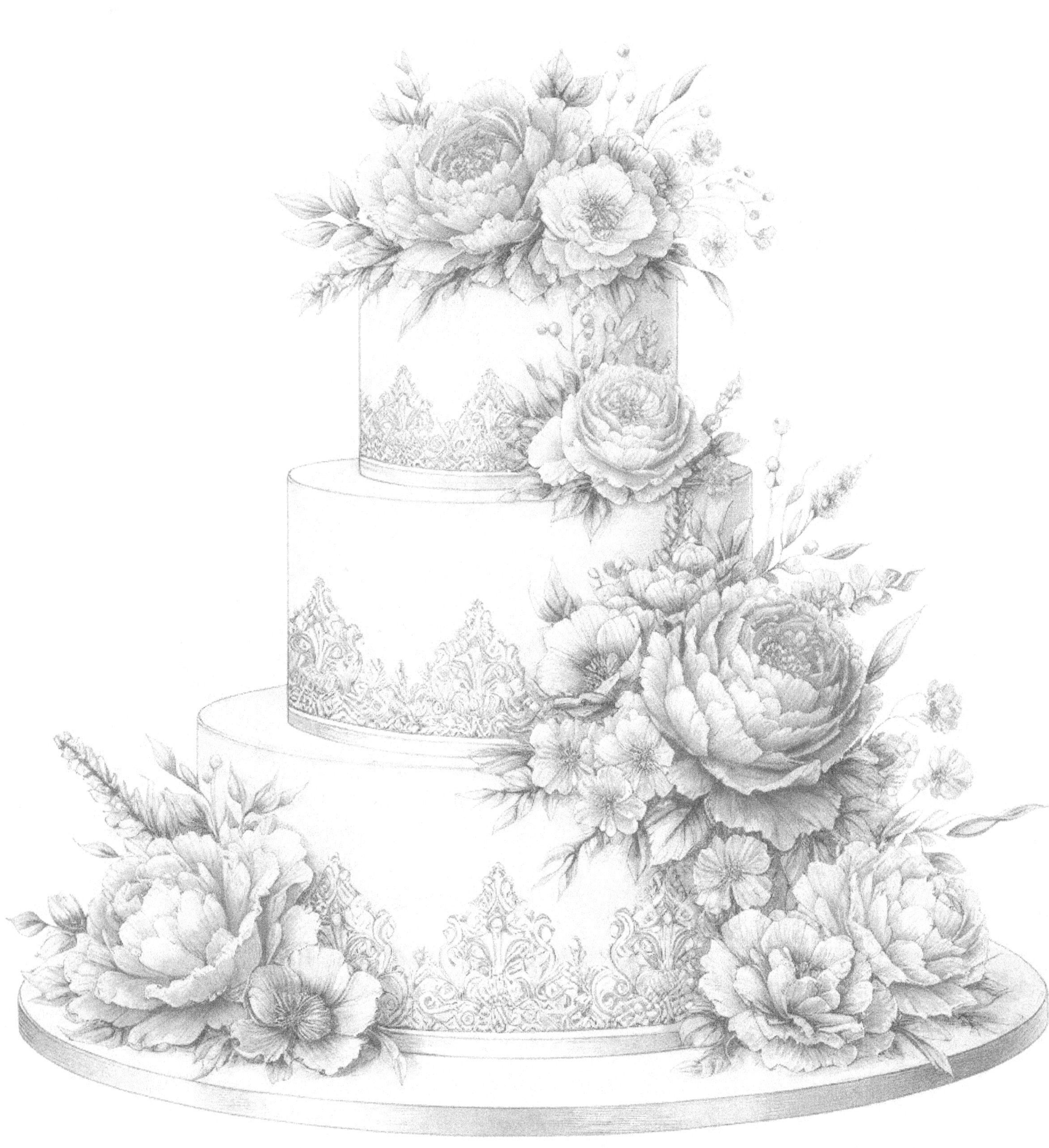

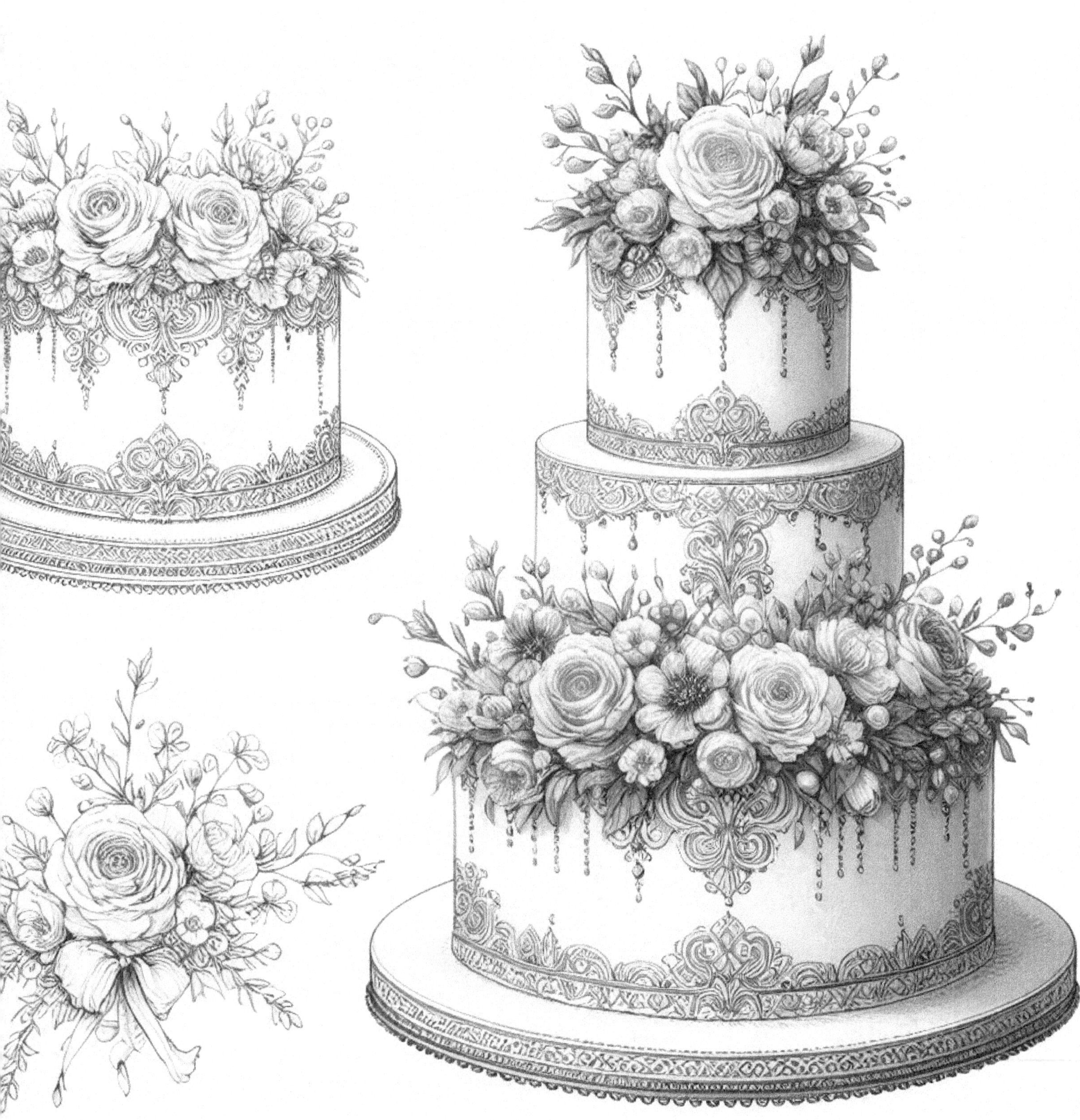

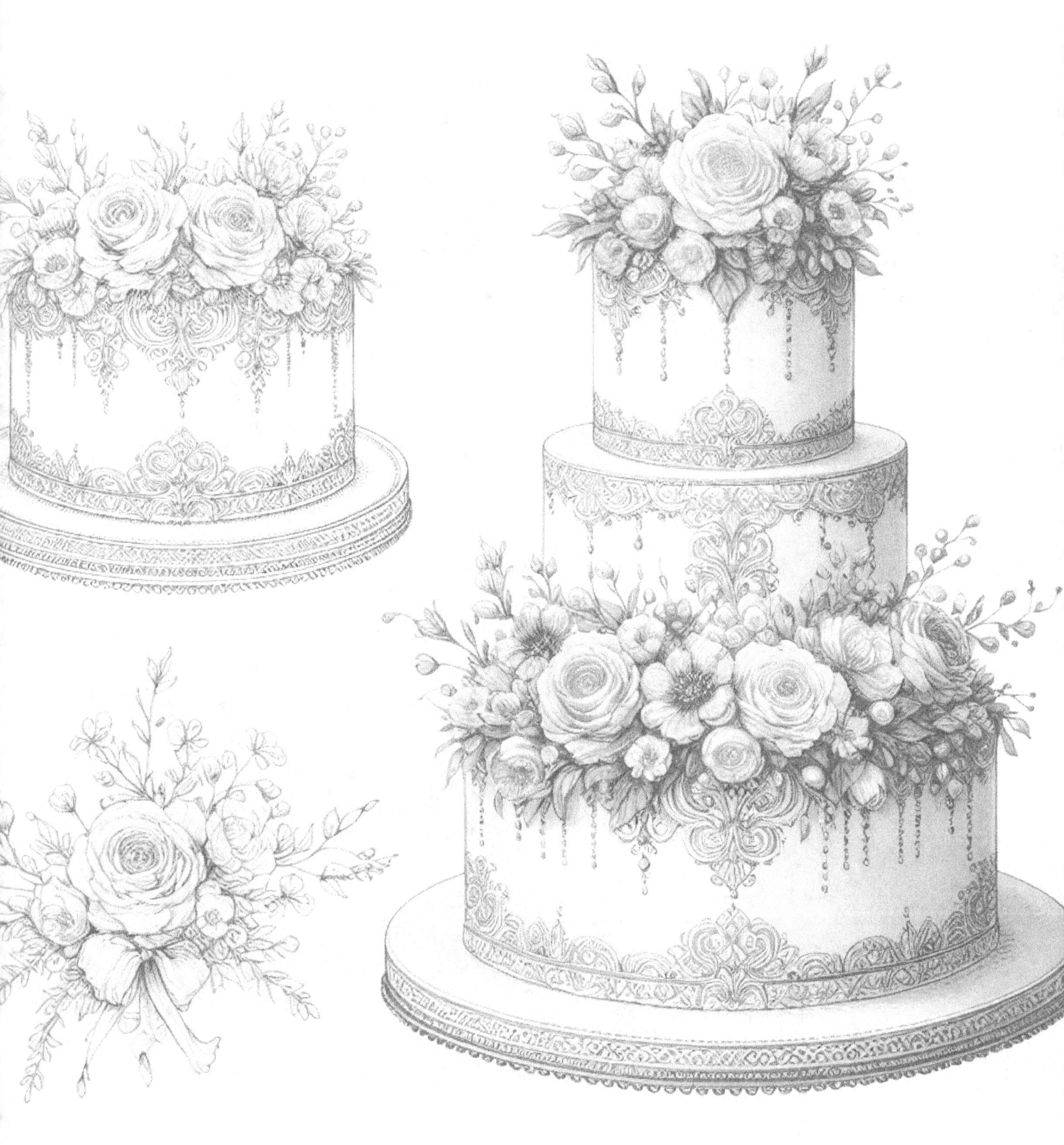

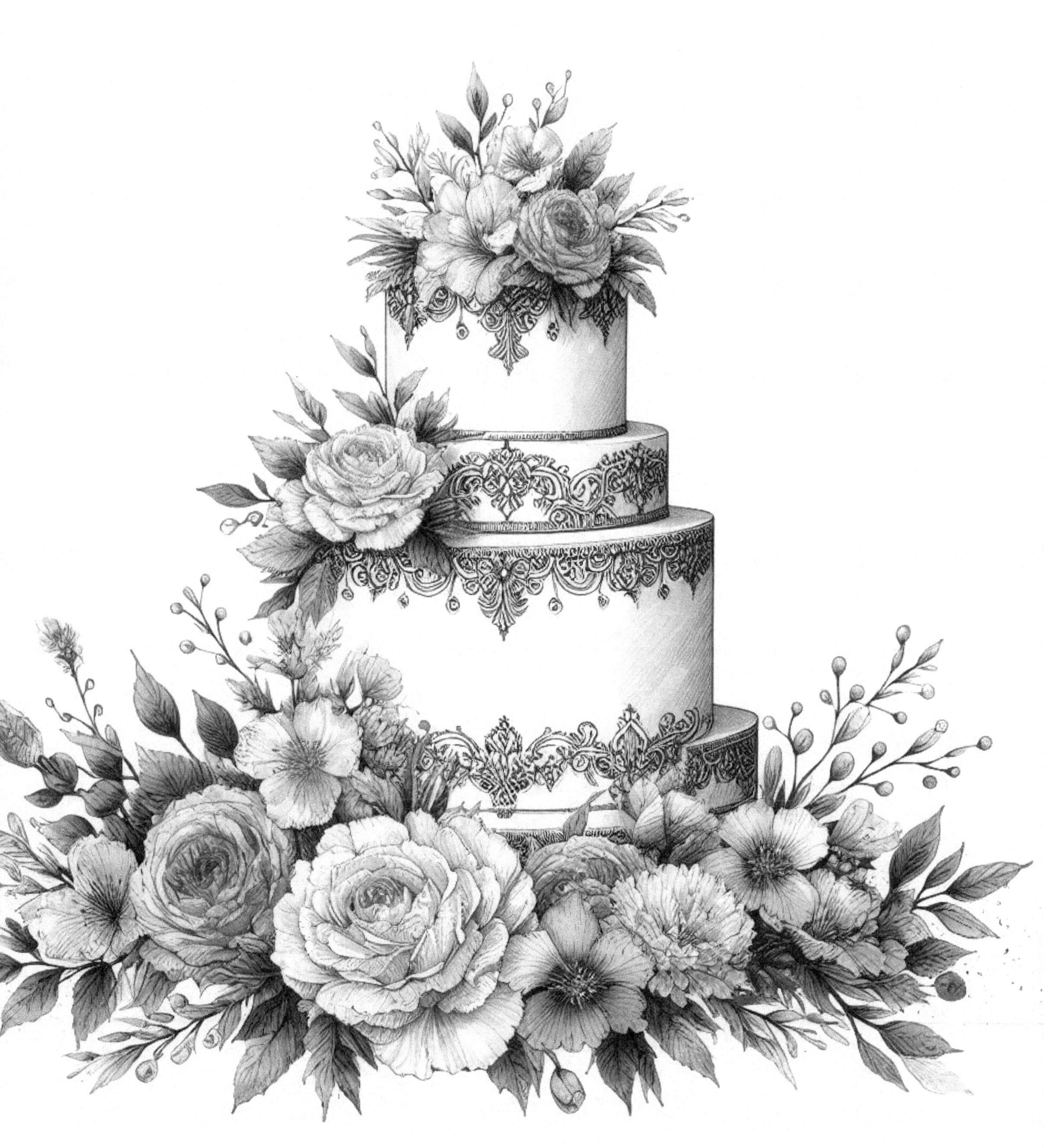

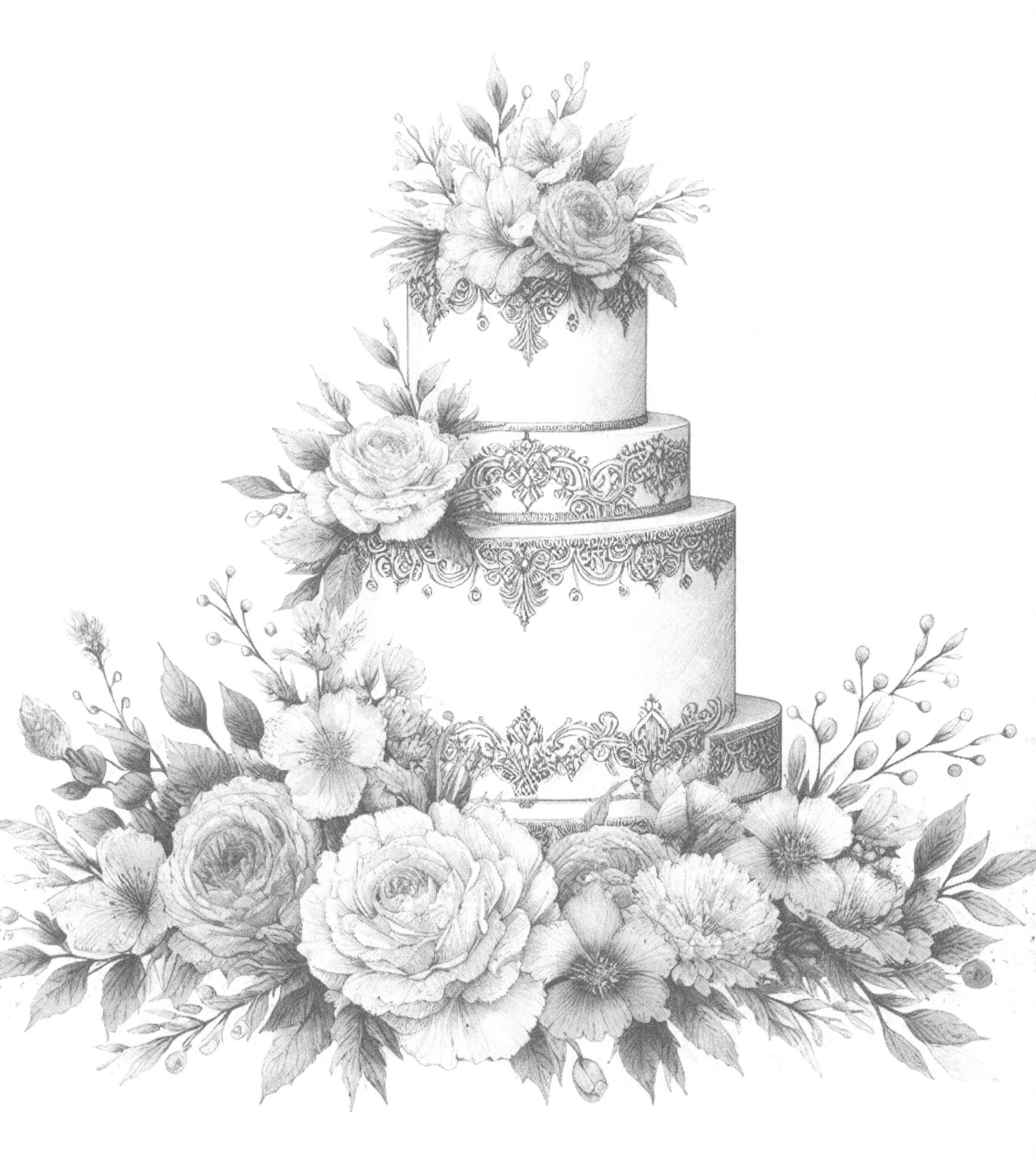

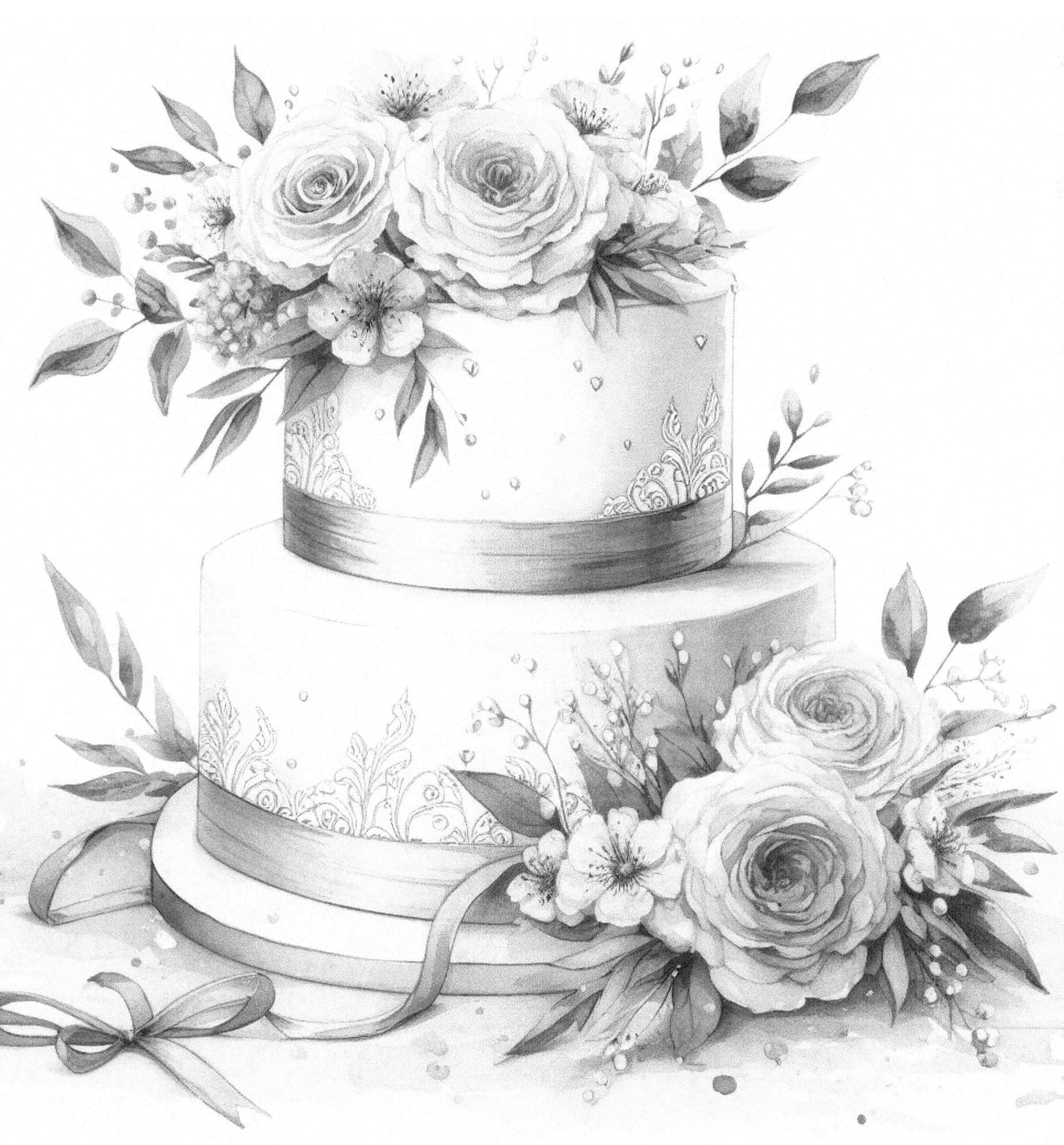

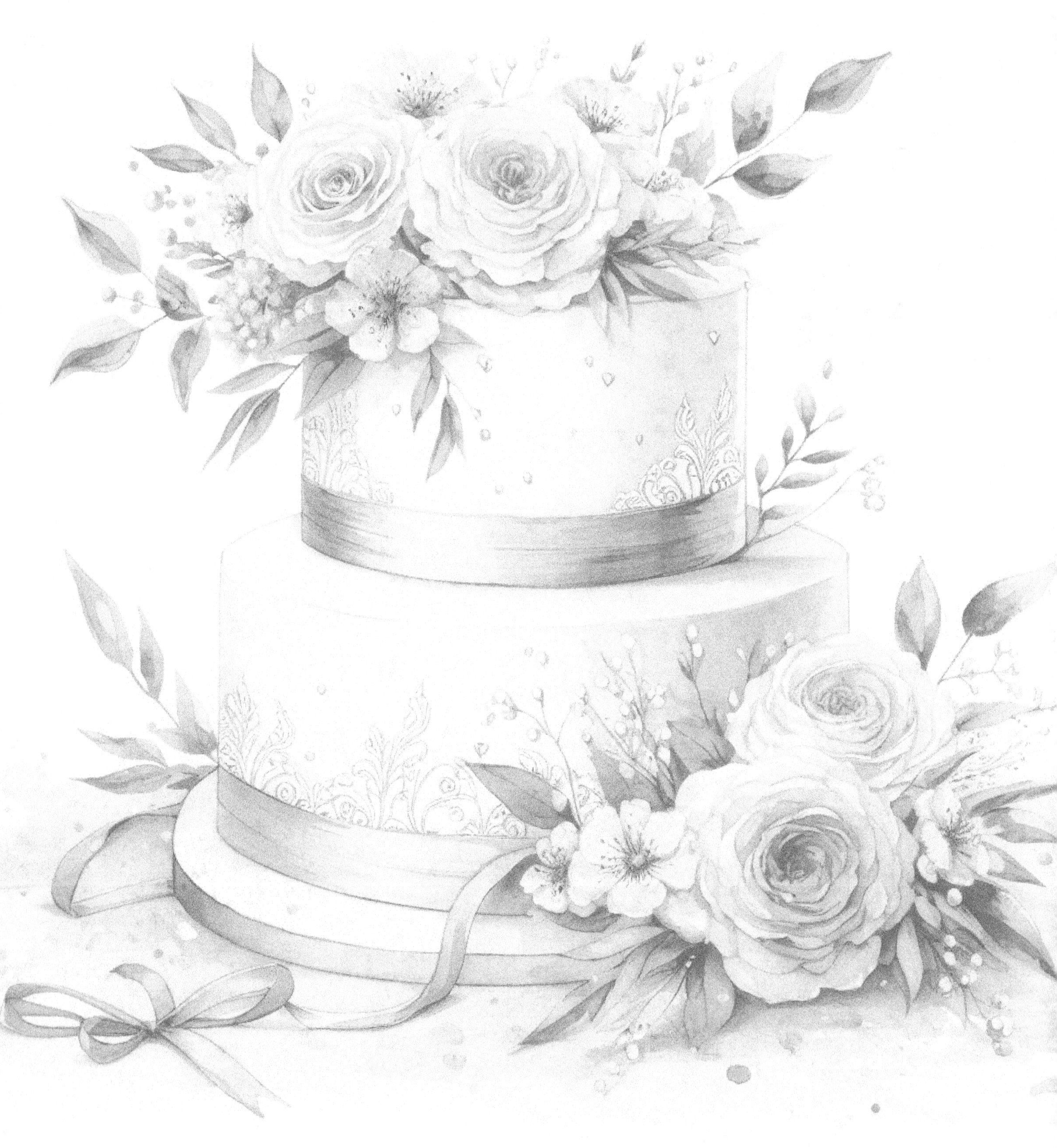

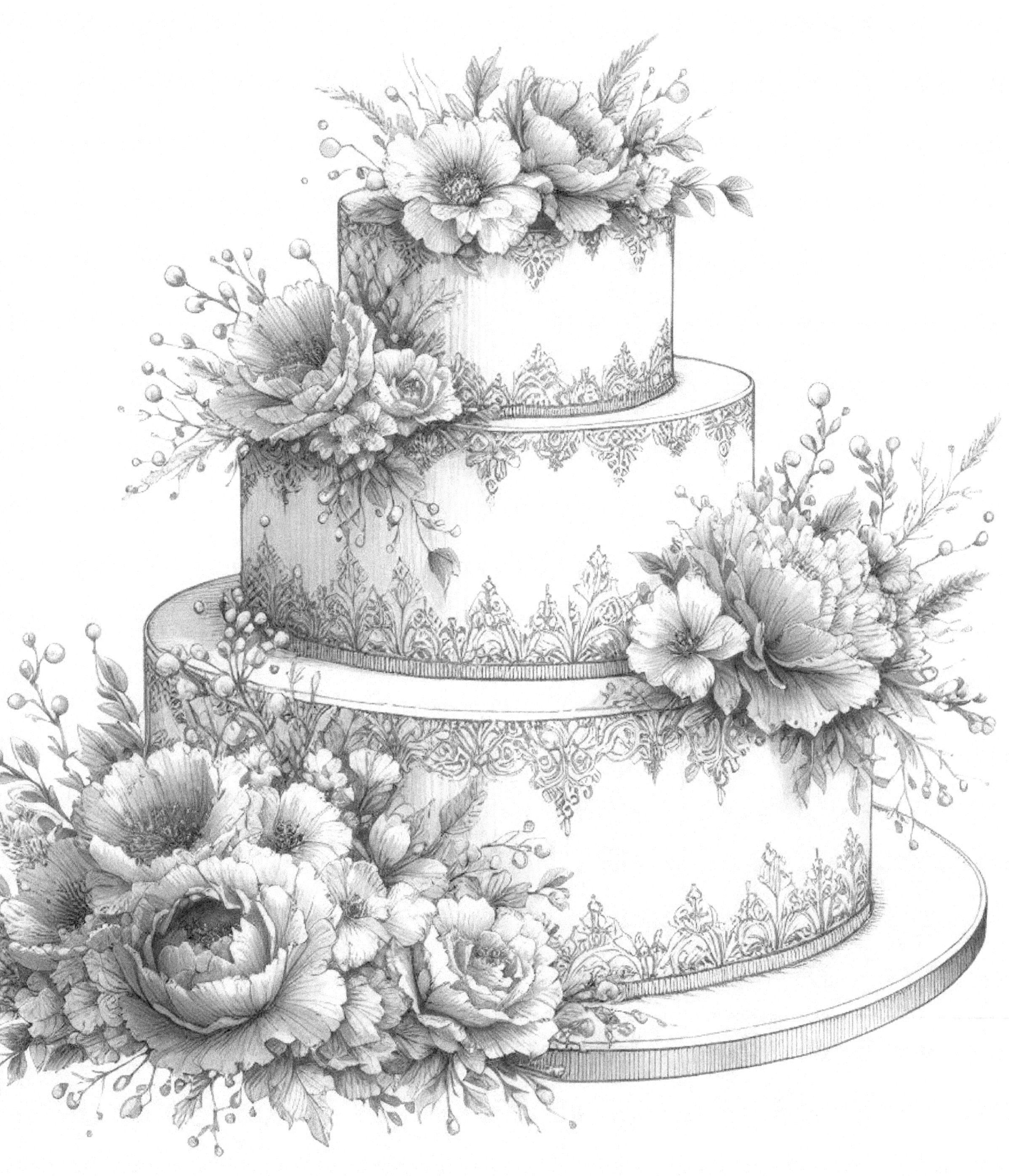

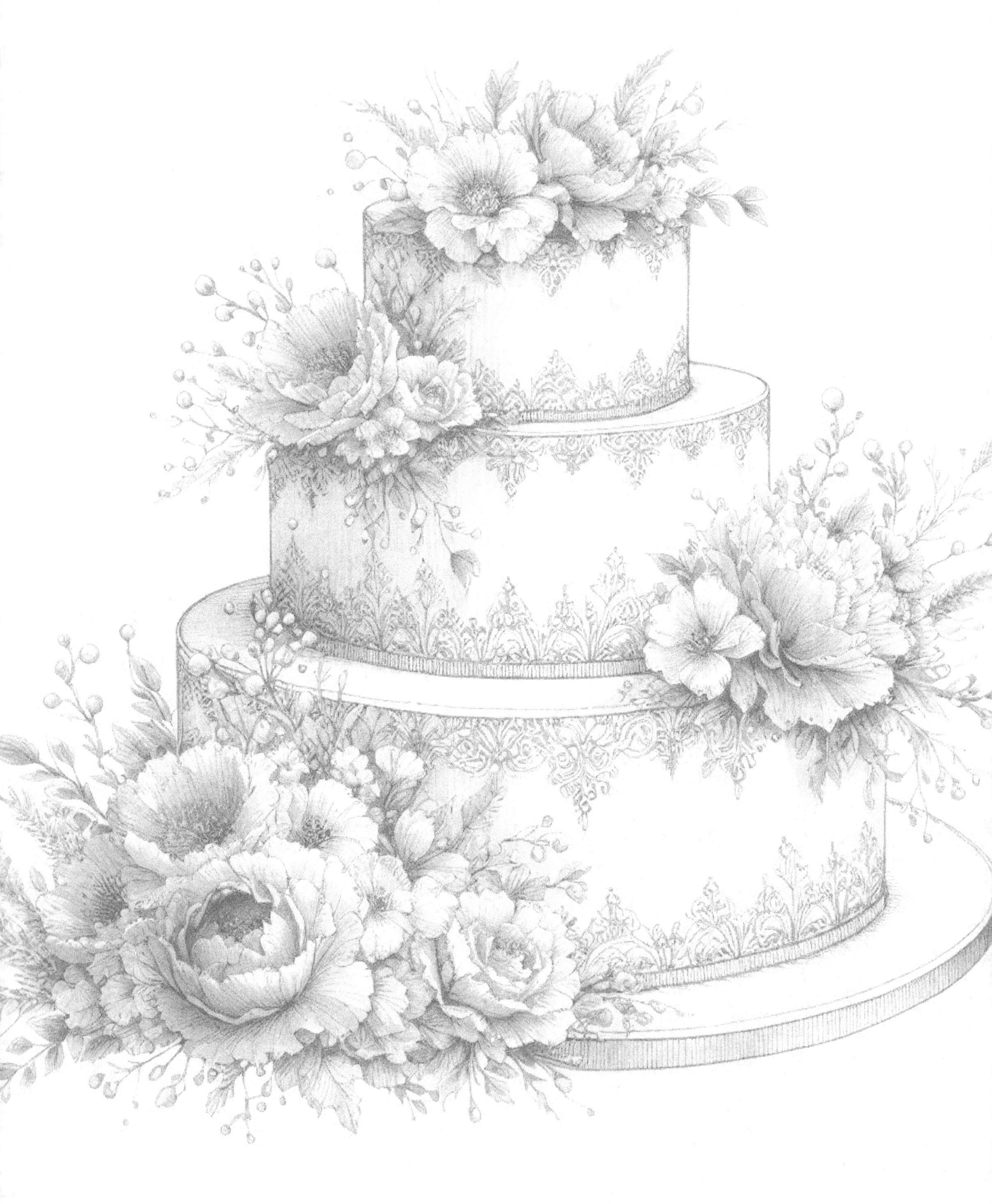

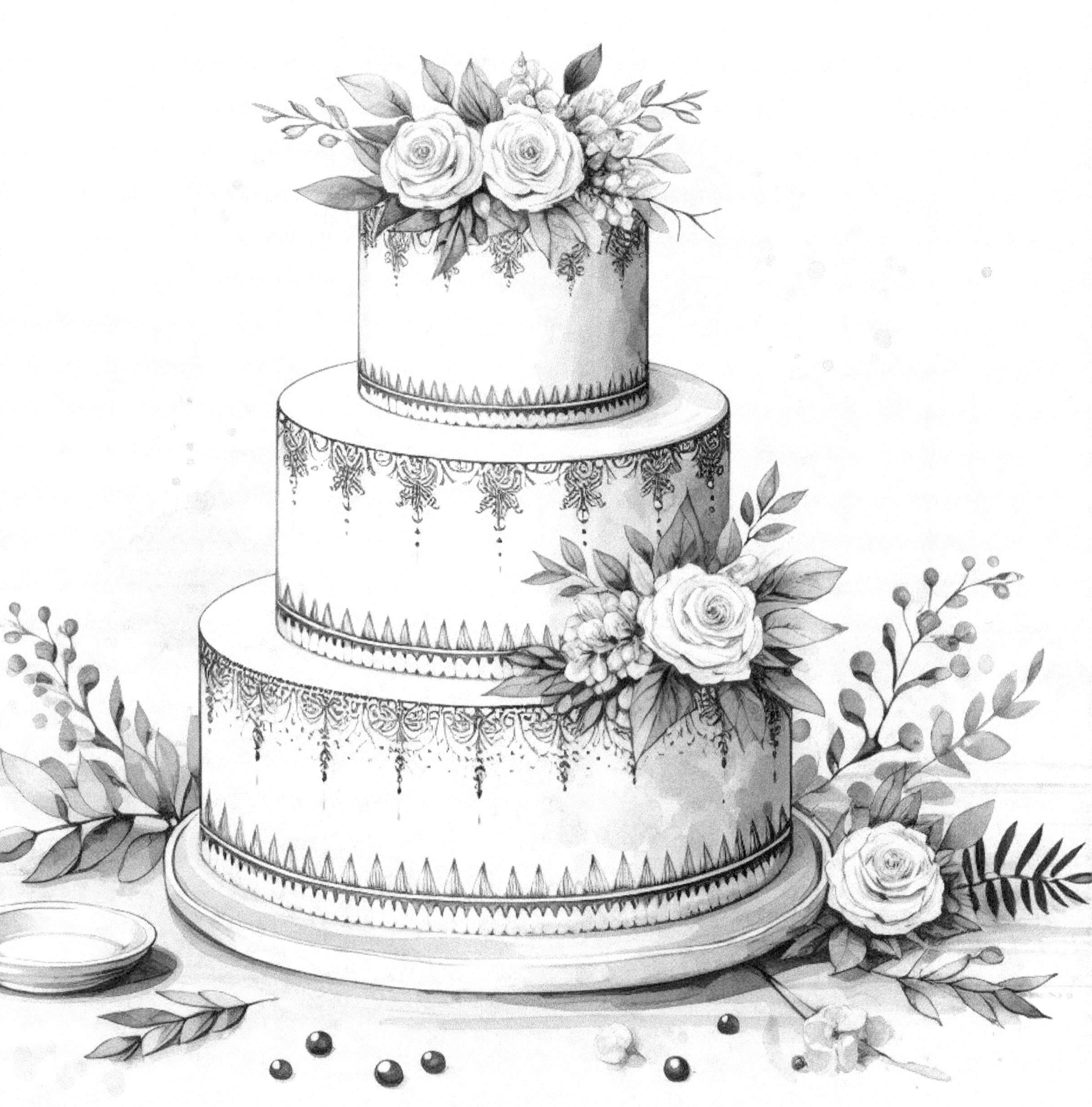

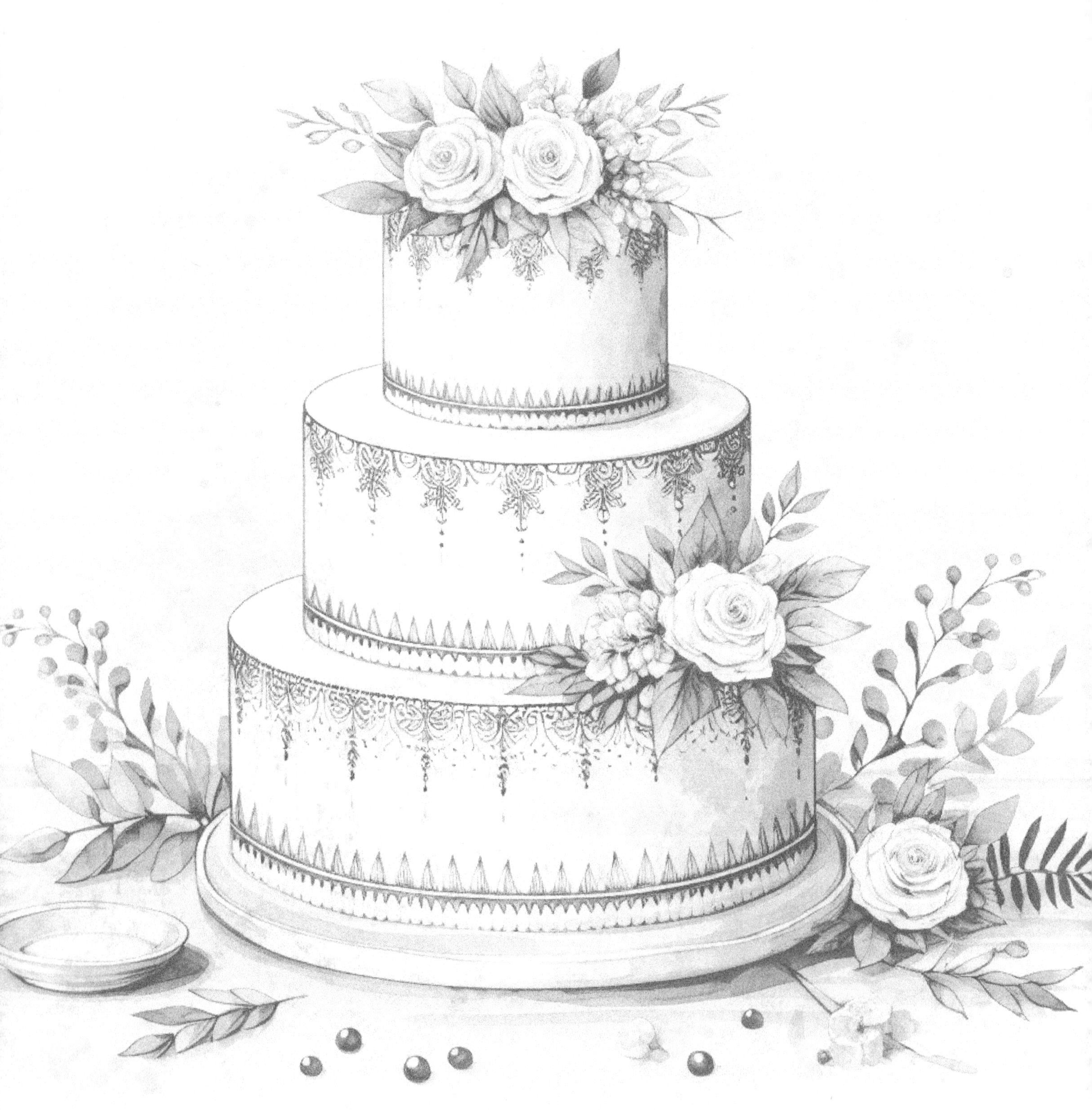

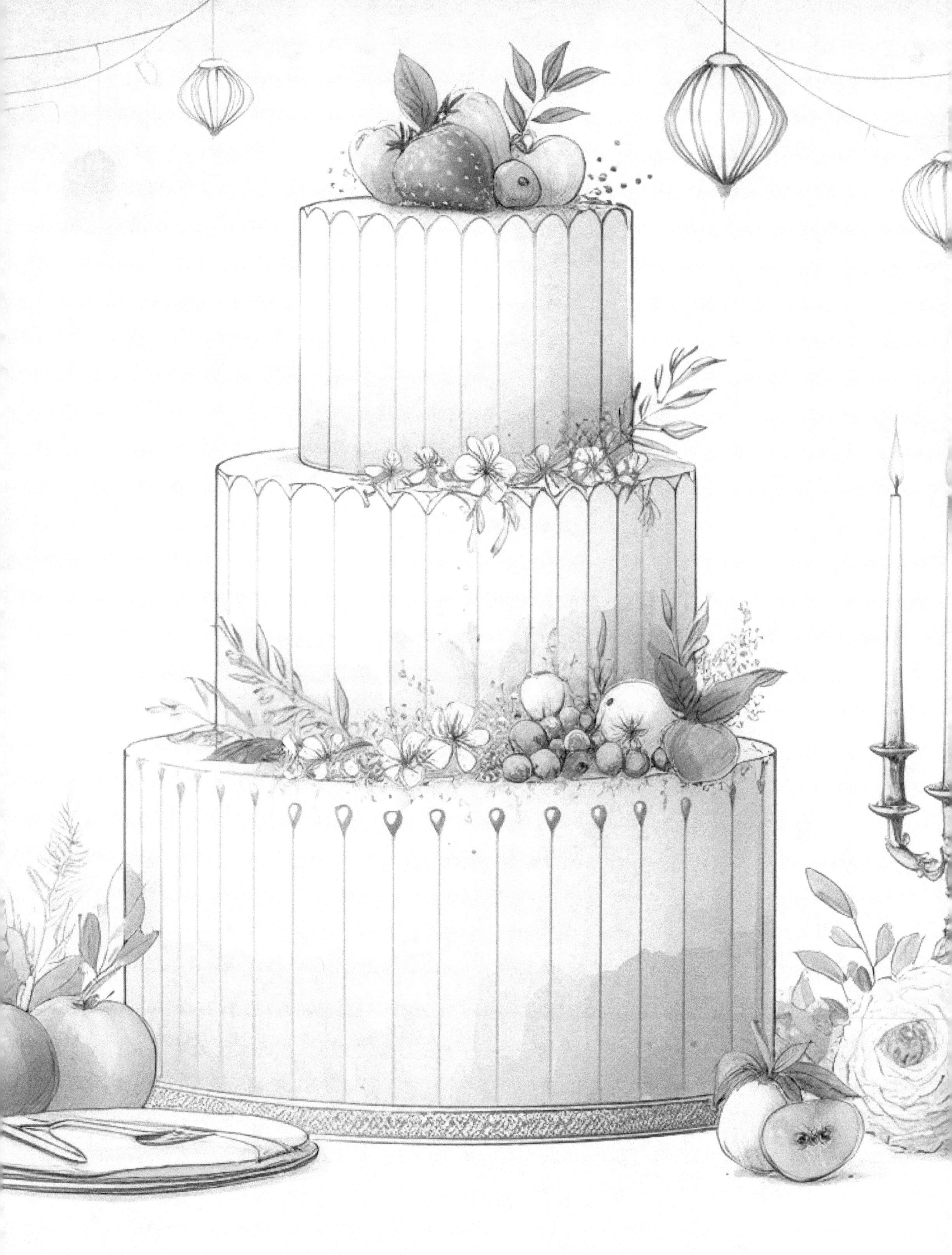

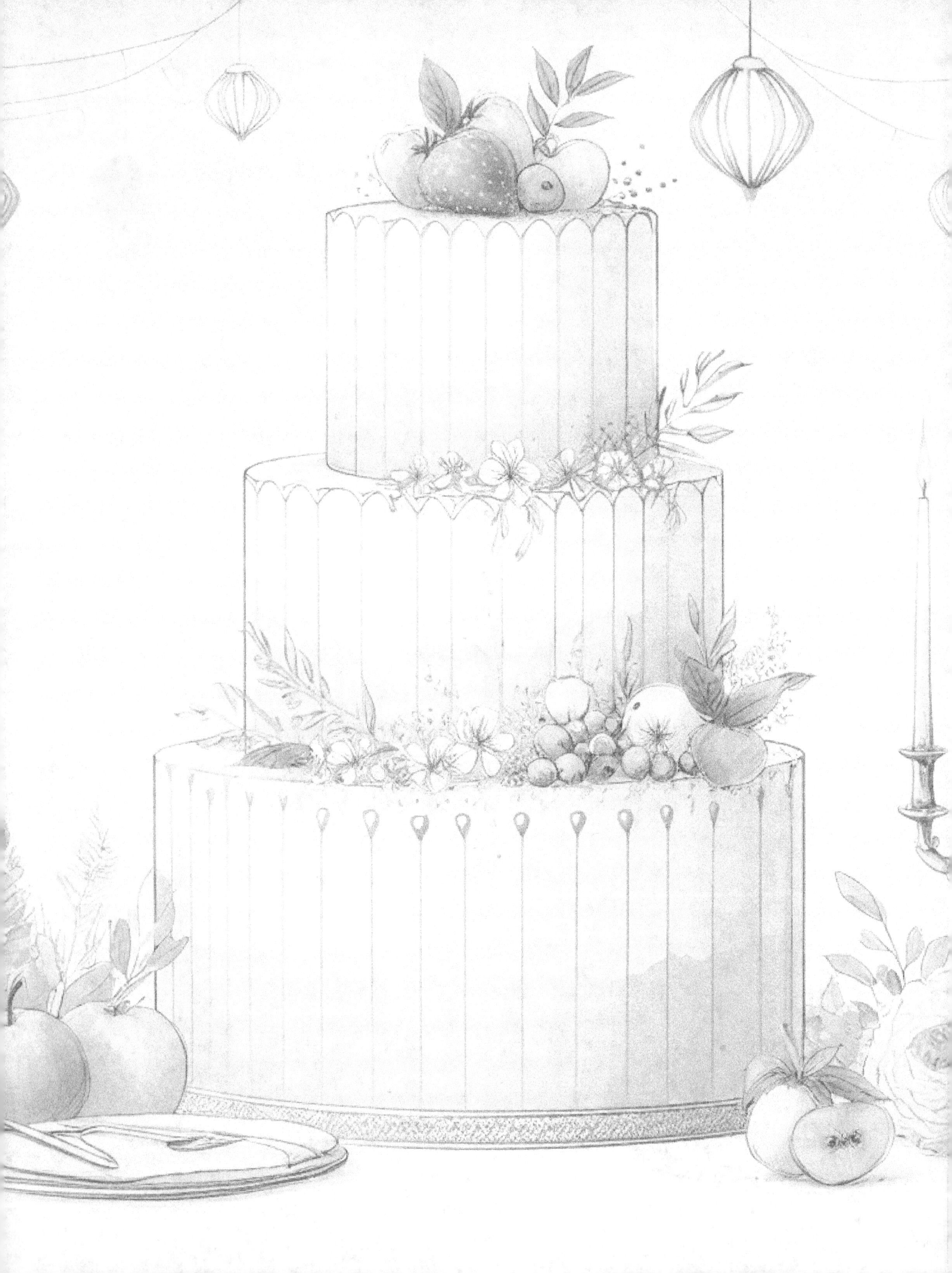

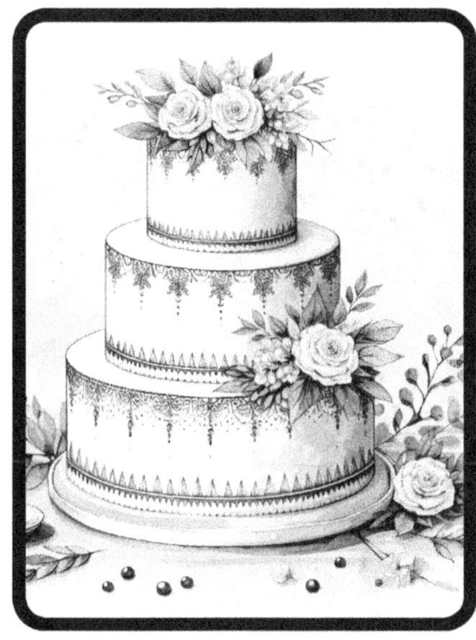
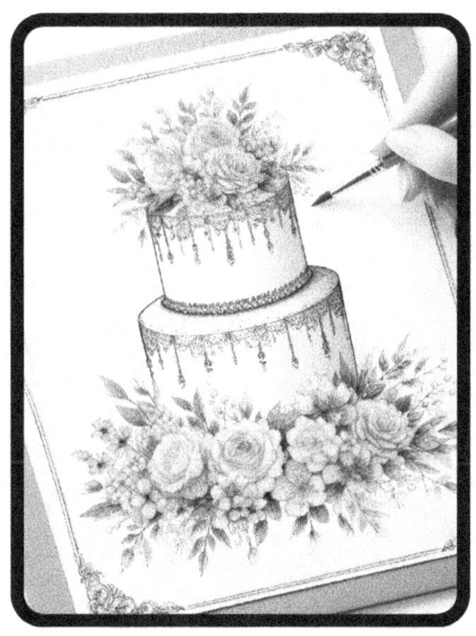
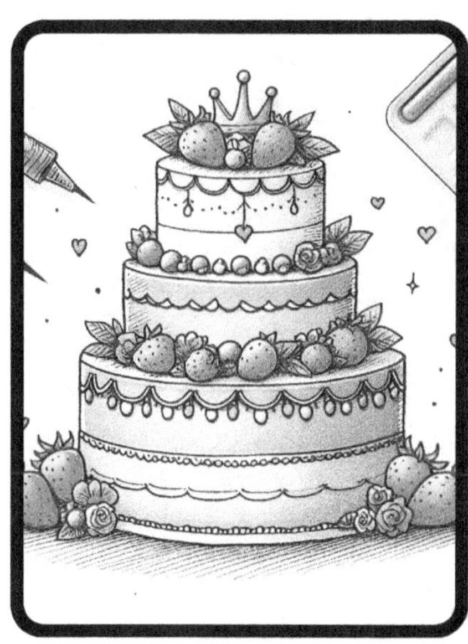
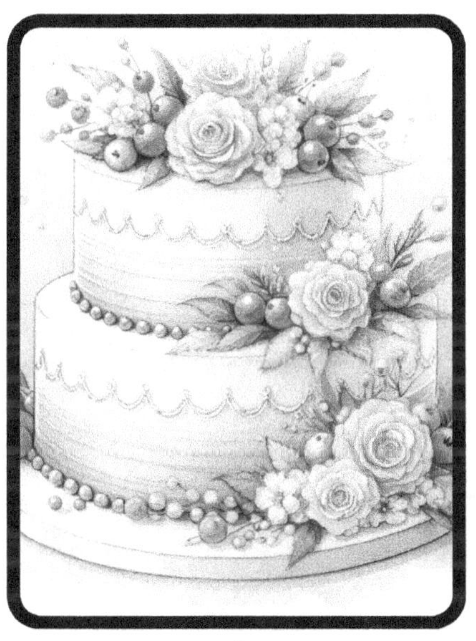
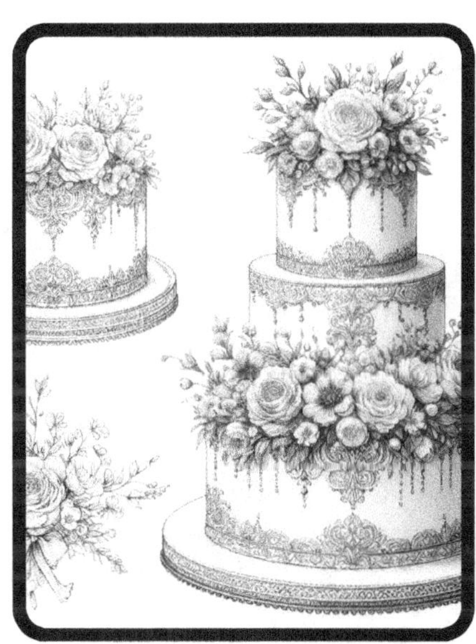
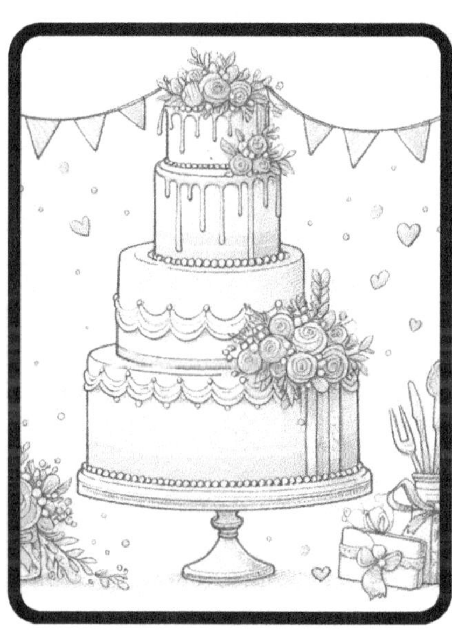
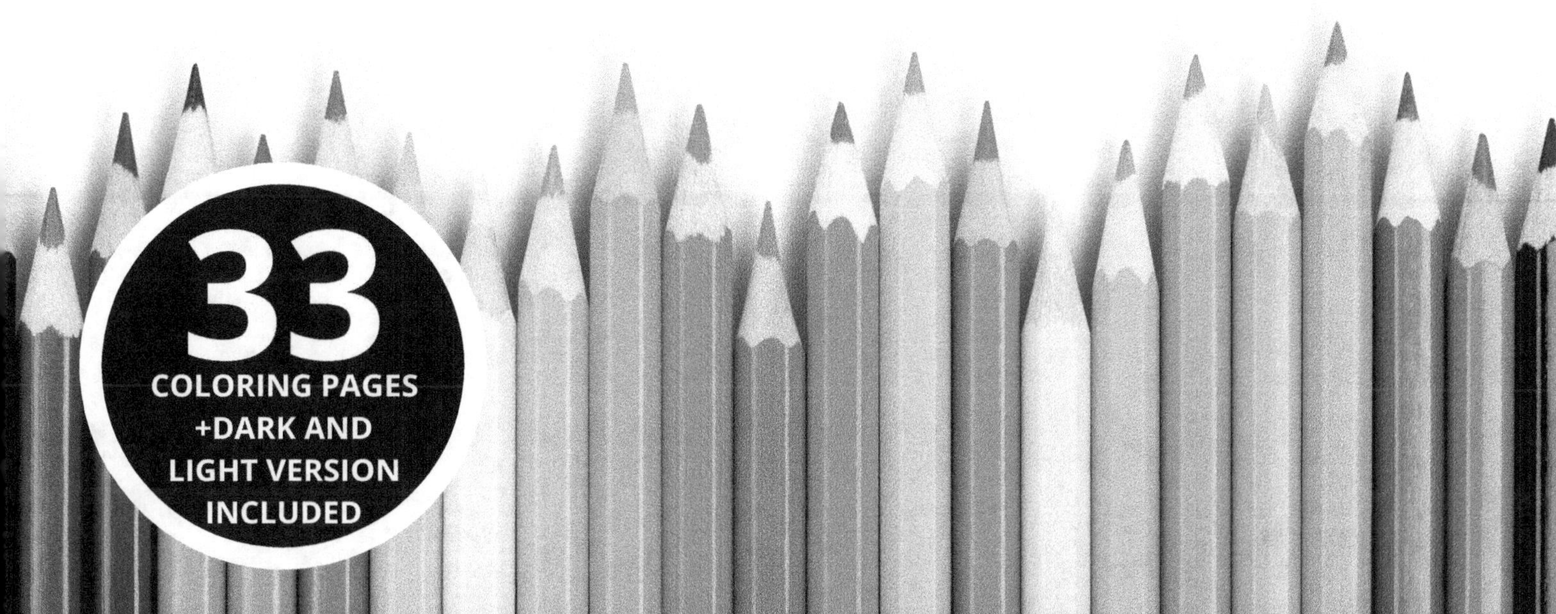
33
COLORING PAGES
+DARK AND
LIGHT VERSION
INCLUDED